1250

Field of Valor

DUTY, HONOR, COUNTRY, AND WINNING THE HEISMAN

Jack Clary

TRIUMPH
BOOKS

CHICAGO

**This book is dedicated to those five men from
Annapolis and West Point who won the Heisman Trophy,
and to their brothers and sisters in arms,
who followed the mandate of Douglas MacArthur:
"On the fields of friendly strife are sown the seeds,
that upon other fields, on other days,
will bear the fruits of victory."**

Library of Congress Cataloging-in-Publication Data

Clary, Jack T.
    Field of valor : duty, honor, country, and winning the Heisman / Jack Clary.
        p. cm.
    Includes index.
    ISBN 1-57243-468-6 (hard)
        1. Football players—United States—Biography. 2. Heisman Trophy. 3. Unites States Military Academy—Football—History. 4. United States Naval Academy—Football—History. I. title.

GV939.A1 C517 2002
796.332'092'2—dc21
[B]

                                                                    2002071963

This book is available in quantity at special discounts for your group or organization. For further information, contact:
Triumph Books
601 South LaSalle Street
Suite 500
Chicago, Illinois, 60605
(312) 939-3330
Fax (312) 663-3557

Printed in the United States of America
ISBN 1-57243-468-6

Interior design by Ray Ramos/Eileen Wagner

Contents

Foreword

"Valor" is a word rooted in the Latin ward *valere*, meaning "to be strong." It often invokes images of courage or fearlessness.

In history, in literature, and in life, valor does not refer to being physically strong or mentally tough. It is more than that. Valor slices through the psyche, elevating one's values and lifting one's emotions to higher levels of aspiration and inspiration. It fires the imagination to great heights, to an absolute conviction that no obstacle is beyond human abilities.

Valor produces the very best combination of one's attributes, generating a synergy in which the whole is greater than the sum of its parts. When valor appears in times of crisis, our true character is laid out for all to see. Hemingway described character as "grace under pressure," and that is what valor calls forth— a maximum and total commitment to the common good when absolutely everything is on the line.

No one shows more true valor than ordinary persons under extraordinary circumstances. At such times, those who assume the mantle of valor often perform beyond even their own expectations. This gives birth to heroes on the battlefield, in competition, and in many other forms of daily life. Most acts of valor are spontaneous and most of those who perform them do not think that they are doing anything out of the ordinary. To them, they are doing nothing more than is reasonable under the circumstances. And that is what truly makes a valorous person.

There were times when our Navy teams had to call upon this quality, either to win or to preserve a victory. When we played Notre Dame in 1960, an apparent victory was suddenly jeopardized very late in the game after the Irish completed a long pass deep into our territory. All that we had fought so hard to attain that day suddenly appeared to be lost as Notre Dame stood poised to score a touchdown and win the game.

My teammates ran down the field after the play in order to form a last-ditch defense, and many of them seemed to be hanging their heads, as if the game were already lost. But something inside me made me look each one of my teammates in the eyes and shout, "Refuse to lose! Refuse to lose!" over and over again.

I didn't do it because of some feeling of bravado, but because I knew that we were good enough, that we had prepared ourselves to cope with any adversity. And it was true—they didn't beat us. We stopped Notre Dame from scoring and we won the game. A photographer caught that moment on film and every time

I look at that photo, it helps me to believe that my insistence on keeping our heads up and battling even harder did have an effect.

Men who perform valorous deeds on the battlefield do so because they feel so confident about their abilities that success is all but preordained. That is because they have been so thoroughly trained and have so much experience using that training that they can make decisions and act instantly, over and above what they normally would do.

Those who rushed into the World Trade Center's Twin Towers in New York City back on September 11, 2001, to save or rescue people trapped in those burning buildings, did so because their training had eradicated any feelings of doubt that they could not succeed. Sadly, factors beyond their control doomed many of their efforts, but the valor they displayed that day united a nation.

Valor, bravery, audacity . . . call it what you will. But remember that it isn't only seen on a battlefield or a playing field. Don't forget that doomed plane over Pennsylvania, deterred from its suicide mission by brave passengers who sacrificed their lives while forcing their hijackers to crash harmlessly into an open field in Pennsylvania and not into the White House or the U.S. Capitol. Indeed, from average men and women such as those come scores of heroes.

And of course we must also never forget the countless others who deliver such virtues in the course of their daily lives. It may not be in a life or death situation but there are those who are willing to step up and take the lead when a key decision must be carried out. What they do is a tribute to their own character and the fact that they have prepared themselves to act in such a noble fashion, without hesitation or the need for applause. They indeed reach the pinnacle of being an All-American, and they are living witnesses that a valorous deed, performed on its own, truly is its own reward.

In that spirit, I dedicate this Foreword to my teammates and shipmates who have shown valor in times of war and in other crises. They are my heroes by virtue of their fortitude, cool-headed determination, and perseverance against all adversity. They inspired themselves and those around them to ignore their human frailties and succeed when others might have succumbed to despair. In so doing, some of them have paid the supreme sacrifice for their efforts; but the memory of their deeds and accomplishments will live forever.

— Joe Bellino
Bedford, Massachusetts

vi

Acknowledgments

I must acknowledge the efforts of several persons who helped me gather information and turn into a readable manuscript what is now *Field of Valor*.

At Annapolis, a special thanks must go to my longtime dear friend Tom Bates, former sports information director at the Naval Academy, who sadly passed away before this book could be published; to assistant athletic director Eric Ruden; and to current sports information director Scott Strassmeier.

At West Point, sports information director Bob Beretta was very helpful; and so were Alicia Mauldin of the archives staff in West Point's library and Col. Herbert Morris (USA, retired) of the West Point Alumni Association. Former All-America player Joe Steffy, a teammate of Glenn Davis and Doc Blanchard, was tireless in getting information for that chapter, and for offering some great insights into the great Army teams from that time.

The counsel of Rudy Riska, who is majordomo of the Heisman Trophy at the Downtown Athletic Club in New York City, was especially helpful in contacting the five subjects of this book; I thank him also for his counsel and for opening his picture files to help illustrate this book.

Pat Harmon, the historian at the College Football Hall of Fame, was his usual cooperative self in digging out information for use in the book.

Good editorial directors and editors are invaluable for a project like this. Thus, at Triumph Books, I salute editorial director Tom Bast; managing editor Blythe Hurley; editorial assistant Bilal Dardai; and freelance editor Dawn Shoemaker, who edited and polished the manuscript.

I also thank the former teammates of the book's five subjects, who so willingly gave of their time to offer reminiscences and other information that was so necessary in putting this book together.

The publisher gratefully acknowledges the assistance of Ltc. Jon A. Torzewski, Sgt. Dan Wakely, and Spc. Jeannine Anderson of the Indiana Army National Guard for their help in preparing the cover photo. Grateful thanks also to Mike Albright at West Point; Ken Mierzejewski at the Naval Academy; Rudy Riska, executive director of the Heisman Memorial Trust Foundation; Bernie Kish, executive director of the College Football Hall of Fame; and Kent Stephens, collections manager of the College Football Hall of Fame.

Introduction

The United States Naval Academy in Annapolis, Maryland, and the United States Military Academy in West Point, New York, are very special schools.

To represent them in any area of endeavor is also special. To represent them on the football field, with all of the tradition that each school has built in over a century of playing that sport, is almost beyond description.

But five of us—Joe Bellino and I at Navy and Glenn Davis, Doc Blanchard, and Pete Dawkins at Army—have been doubly honored to have been awarded the Heisman Trophy for our feats during a single season of our football careers at these schools.

When we look back at those years and those seasons, what we seem to remember most are not the plays, runs, and passes, but everything that went into making those teams and those times so unique. There were coaches who took us as young men barely out of high school and taught us not only how to be better football players but, by extension, how to become future military officers in the best tradition of our renowned institutions and the armed services they represented. And there were the teammates whose efforts directed us toward the success that we achieved to warrant the Heisman Trophy. When I received my award, I said that I wished I could have cut up that statue into equal pieces and presented each of my teammates with one, to recognize all they did to contribute to my honor that day.

The five of us who won the Heisman Trophy while playing at either Annapolis or West Point learned before we ever stepped on the football field that we were supported by a 12th man—the Brigade of Midshipmen or the Corps of Cadets. They were our support systems and we played for them more than we played for ourselves. When we succeeded, they succeeded; when we didn't, neither did they.

One of the greatest things about winning the Heisman Trophy was the pride that it brought to our Navy football team in 1963 and to the entire class of 1965 at the Naval Academy. It was not my trophy; it was the team's trophy and my class's trophy. It is that way today and it will be that way until the last one of us is gone.

I am certain that each of the four other Heisman Trophy winners feels the same way. All of them were great players but the one message they have consistently tried to express through the years (as have I) is that the award represented the excellence of every member of the team. We are just custodians; our teammates and our classmates are co-owners. We were all imbued with the concept of team over self—there is no "I" in *team*.

When reading about heroes and valor, the one thing that becomes apparent is that all such people and all such deeds are done in the cause of benefiting others. There is no "I" in *valor*, either.

This selfless spirit has been the model, for more than a century, which players from both schools have followed as they have willingly engaged, when asked, in the defense of their country. Scores of former football players at both schools have been as heroic on the battlefield as they were on the football field. Their valorous deeds would fill several volumes and one never really tires of hearing of the extraordinary feats that they performed even though their own lives were often at risk.

In the past year many parallels have been drawn between soldiers in our armed forces and the actions of the brave police, firemen, and rescue personnel involved in the horrific events that marked the attacks on the World Trade Center in New York City, the Pentagon in Washington, and the hijacked airliner over Pennsylvania on September 11, 2001. By extension, the passengers aboard that hijacked plane, which was earmarked by its captors to destroy one of our great buildings in Washington, certainly belong among the pantheon of heroes from that horrible day. Those unarmed civilians, knowing they were doomed, nonetheless fought back and prevented that plane from completing its horrendous mission. They crashed and died in an open field in Pennsylvania, every bit as heroic as anyone from either the Naval Academy or the Military Academy who ever was killed on a battlefield.

In this book, the five of us are celebrated for the things that we did to earn the Heisman Trophy. But more importantly, others within the book's covers who also share the football traditions at our schools, as well as the uncelebrated heroes around us all, are celebrated for what they did in defense of their country on countless fields of valor.

— **Roger Staubach**
Dallas, Texas

x

Field of Valor

DUTY, HONOR, COUNTRY, AND WINNING THE HEISMAN

Chapter 1
Joe Bellino

In Sicilian, the word *bellino* means "little beauty."

In terms of the history of the Heisman Trophy and the football traditions of the Naval Academy, that meaning was a perfect fit for Joe Bellino; he was indeed a "little beauty" on the football field. But his beauty as a player was so much bigger and more powerful than the 187 pounds so perfectly sculpted over his 5'9" frame and tucked into his now-retired No. 27 jersey.

From 1958 through 1960, Bellino's football achievements elevated him to the pinnacle of all the running backs who had preceded him at the Naval Academy. In the 80 years of its football history to that time, Navy had established a great tradition of producing stellar runners—players such as Fred "Buzz" Borries, Steve Barchet, Tom Hamilton, Barnacle Bill Busik, Bobby Jenkins, Fred Franco, Joe Gattuso Sr., and Ned Oldham. When Bellino finished playing in 1960, he stood atop that list after climaxing his career by becoming the first Navy player ever to win the Heisman Trophy.

To win the Heisman is to be acclaimed as college football's greatest individual player for a particular season. No other award in sports is so significant and so unique. When Bellino won it, though, it was just one small part of his life at that time, a life that was being directed day and night for four years toward performing on a battlefield in the same measure as he had performed on the playing field.

Those who do that above and beyond the call of duty are awarded the Medal of Honor, the nation's highest award for heroism. In a metaphorical sense only, the Medal of Honor is to a warrior what the Heisman Trophy is to a college football player.

There have been more than 70 men in the history of the navy who have won the Medal of Honor, and six of them have been former Navy football players. One of them was Richard Nott Antrim, a fine running back like Bellino who played on the 1930 team. There was no Heisman Trophy to honor players like Antrim, so he was rewarded only by his teammates. Twelve years later, and nearly twenty years before Bellino's exploits, Antrim's football achievements paled in significance to what he achieved while he was a Japanese prisoner of war.

In April 1942, Antrim was captured by the Japanese after they sank his destroyer, the USS *Pope*. The prison camp guards were brutal jailers who forced the prisoners to live in subhuman conditions that included daily beatings for even the most minute infraction, or even at the whim of the guards. Conditions were deteriorating so badly in 1943 that the 2,700 prisoners, mostly U.S. Navy personnel, were willing to risk death to try to overthrow their jailers.

One day, while seeing a fellow officer continually beaten even after he had lapsed into unconsciousness, Antrim could stand it no more. "Let him alone," he

Midshipman Bellino.

Stu Whelan

Richard Antrim.

screamed. "If you want to beat someone, then beat me. Can't you see he's nearly dead?"

The Japanese guards were so stunned that they stopped beating the prisoner. But Antrim's startling display of bravery so cowed them that they were afraid of him, too, and didn't touch him. His action not only led the camp commander to impose better living conditions but it blunted the possible revolt in which most of the prisoners in the camp would have been slaughtered. For his heroism Antrim was awarded the Medal of Honor and added the Navy Cross, Bronze Star, and Purple Heart to a litany of other awards he had earned. He survived the war and later retired as a rear admiral.

Yet heroism, like great football play, isn't always acknowledged by supreme awards. Gordon Underwood, a guard on Antrim's 1930 team, commanded the submarine USS *Spadefish*. Working in a "wolf pack" (a group of submarines making a coordinated attack) on his first patrol, his boat sank nearly 29,000 tons of Japanese shipping. During a second command aboard the USS *Queenfish*, Underwood's wolf pack ran into a Japanese force trying to reinforce troops in the Philippines. His boat sank an aircraft carrier while the rest of the wolf pack decimated the convoy's other ships. While on the surface recharging the boat's batteries after the battle, Underwood and the *Queenfish* were attacked by a couple of Japanese sub chasers. The *Queenfish* managed to submerge, and Underwood then attacked his pursuers with four torpedoes—and heard three explosions.

Underwood's actions were in the finest Navy tradition, and the fleet has carried ample testimony to the fact by the numbers of its ships that are named after war heroes. Many of those war heroes, such as Antrim and Underwood, also were football players who will always have a share in the glories achieved by those in later generations. It started with Worth Bagley, a four-year letterman at Annapolis in the early 1890s. He scored one touchdown and kicked two field goals to help defeat

Bellino made the most spectacular catch of his career in the 1961 Orange Bowl. Unfortunately Navy lost to Missouri 21–14.

Army in 1892. Seven years later, he was the first United States naval officer killed in action in the Spanish-American War, losing his life on the USS *Winslow* during an attack on gun batteries in Cardenas, Cuba.

Bellino and all of his football-playing brethren at the Naval Academy knew then—as their successors know today—that life-threatening situations would be distinct possibilities during their naval careers. They were a much higher calling than the gridiron glories that seemed so glamorous and that brought such adulation, particularly in the era during which Bellino played, when the teams and the players at both Annapolis and West Point were consistently among the finest in the nation.

Bellino, and later another Navy player, Roger Staubach, came along at the tail end of a football glory run by both academies. In 1958, two years before Bellino won the Heisman, Army's Pete Dawkins had become the third West Point player in 12 years to win the award. He had been preceded by the inimitable duo of Felix "Doc"

Eddie Erdelatz.

Blanchard in 1945 and Glenn Davis in 1946. Even after Blanchard and Davis graduated, Army football teams were nationally ranked; their players dotted All-America teams and later performed heroically on the battlefields of Korea and Vietnam.

Another high point in Navy's football revival was marked by Bellino's excellence as a player. During World War II, Navy had competed with Army for the national championship, then struggled until Eddie Erdelatz became Navy's head coach in 1950. He helped make it one of the fifties' most successful college football programs. Navy's famed 1954 "Team Named Desire," quarterbacked by George Welsh and featuring a couple of future Marine Corps generals, team captain Phil Monahan and tackle John Hopkins, had captivated an entire nation with its gutsy play for an entire season. Their heroics were capped when they won the 1955 Sugar Bowl with a 21–0 victory over favored Mississippi.

Three years later the 1957 team, using something it called the "jitterbug defense," defeated Army and Dawkins, 14–0, and then capped its success with a 20–7 victory over Rice in the Cotton Bowl. It is said that the toughest player that Navy team faced all year was a running back on its own plebe (freshman) team named Joe Bellino.

Bellino was a special player, as he proved throughout his 1960 Heisman season. He was a first-team selection on every major All-America list, won the prestigious Maxwell Award, was selected as the Outstanding College Football Player of

7

Bellino accepting the 1961 Tea Industry Award, which he was awarded for "exemplary standards in physical training and for outstanding contributions to football and the world of sports."

the Year, and received a blizzard of other awards. Before he graduated from the Naval Academy in June 1961, he was the first Navy athlete in 41 years to receive the Academy's two top athletic awards, the Thompson Trophy and the Naval Academy Athletic Association Sword. In 1977 he was inducted into the College Football Hall of Fame.

Navy coach Wayne Hardin had designed his offense in 1960 to take advantage of Bellino's incredible talents, and Bellino soon owned nearly every major statistical record in leading Navy to a 9–1 record and a berth in the Orange Bowl. In that game he scored a touchdown with a diving end zone pass reception and was the game's dominant back, despite the Mids' 21–14 loss to Missouri.

As a running back, Bellino was a throwback to the times when great halfbacks were talked about as being "triple threats." He was one of them because he could run, catch, throw, kick, and play defense. His records abounded: a season rushing mark in his Heisman year of 834 yards became part of his three-season career mark (1,664), which in turn became part of a then-record 3,117 yards of total offense. More than 40 years after his final game, Bellino's 5.04 rushing average still is first in Navy history and has been strong enough to withstand the onslaughts of two other great Navy runners, Eddie Meyers and Napoleon McCallum.

During his three varsity seasons, his numbers tell a large part of his accomplishments: 31 touchdowns (5 in three games against Army) that helped produce 198 points, 45 pass receptions for 620 yards, nearly 20 yards per punt return, and almost 22 yards per kickoff return. His punting ability, while not a full-time occupation, became a weapon when Navy surprised opponents with quick kicks. He also played as a full-time defensive back in the days of single-platoon football.

Without a doubt, Bellino was the most electrifying runner to play for Navy since Buzz Borries in the early thirties. He bedeviled opposing defenses with his speed, balance, and power, plus his ability to change pace while running at top speed. His running style once was likened to "a berserk butterfly that happened to grow up to weigh 187 pounds."

Contrary to public and media perceptions at the time, Bellino did not have blinding speed; it only appeared that way from what he achieved using his unique running style. How fast was he? "Always as fast as he has to be," Hardin repeatedly answered when asked the question.

The only time someone put him "on the clock" in college, he ran the 100-meter dash in 10.9 seconds. But he did that after stepping off the cruiser USS *Northampton* following 17 days at sea where a rolling deck precluded any running. Besides, a football player's speed is measured over 40 yards, not 100 meters. So, no one, not even Joe himself, knew how fast he was in "football time."

However, when Bellino was being pursued by major league baseball scouts, Eddie Pellegrini of the Red Sox once timed him in the 30 yards from home plate to first base and said, "Joe, I've never seen anyone get from home to first as fast as you."

The speed question built up a mystique, and while Bellino certainly was faster than most running backs at the time, the way he ran was the key to his success. He

Bellino's explosive speed helped make him the greatest running back in Navy history.

Joe Bellino.

was the master of changing speeds to fit any situation. He had a unique ability to use bursts of speed to elude or escape would-be tacklers, or to begin a play by slashing through the line of scrimmage before the defense could react. After that, he became a truly dangerous runner because he made defenders look foolish in the open field. They often found themselves grasping at air as he slipped and slithered his way through them. About the only time they ever saw his true speed was when he was in sight of the goal line and turned on his own personal afterburners to get into the end zone.

Still, it wasn't all speed and slithery runs with Bellino. He had massive 18-inch calves, bigger than some men's thighs, which provided the power to break tackles as well as to run through packed defenses. Those powerful legs exploded a fury of force that tore apart a lackadaisical tackler's grasp and sent him reeling to the ground, wondering just what happened. Even dedicated tacklers often found their efforts lacking when Bellino's legs ripped apart their arms and stomped them into the ground. Those legs made him a fine short-yardage runner between the tackles when Navy needed two or three yards for a first down or a touchdown. It took a hard, direct tackle to knock him off his feet because, one of his coaches at the time explained, "With those legs, Joe is bottom-heavy. You knock him up in the air, he's got to come down on his feet."

Steve Belichick, who was Bellino's backfield coach, said, "He was the kind of runner who makes good coaches look like great coaches. He had qualities you don't teach a player—great sense of timing, exceptional balance, and great field vision, particularly peripheral vision that allowed him to see potential tacklers to his side before he decided to move in either direction.

"Joe's speed always sprung him loose," Belichick continued. "You couldn't ask for a back with more tools. He may have weighed only 180 pounds, but he was strong enough to pick up short yardage because he could hit a tackler harder than a tackler could hit him. I always defied any man to stop him in the open field. He had those big legs, but he was so nimble, like a dancer."

Hardin once noted: "It was the way that he ran that made him appear to be running so fast. It was deceptive, but defenses could never cope with it."

In fact, until the final game of his career, in 1960 against Army, he had never been caught from behind at any level of competition. It finally happened on a quick trap play that Navy called on its own 1-yard line to move away from its end zone. Bellino, lined up in the end zone, got the ball and shot through the middle of Army's defense after dodging two defenders who just missed tackling him for a safety. He was past the Cadets' linebackers before he reached the 10-yard line and, instead of getting the few yards for which the play was principally designed, he suddenly had an open field to Army's end zone, some 90 yards away. Paul Stanley, Army's fastest player, finally caught him at the Cadets 41-yard line, 60 yards from where that play began.

It had looked like a perfectly executed play, but every Navy player—except Bellino and quarterback Hal Spooner—missed his assignment. It was Bellino's ability to make those first two Army defenders miss him before he reached the line of scrimmage that was the key to his success. Ironically, had he run from anywhere around midfield, he would have zoomed right into Army's end zone, and his reputation for never having been caught from behind would have remained unsullied.

Tacklers claimed that Bellino ran faster sideways than he did going forward, like a frightened crab. He would start as if launched from a catapult and then kick in his incredible series of speed changes. Some of his longest runs came after he was handed the ball and then bounced around a bit looking for an opening before speeding away.

Sometimes Bellino even brought the defenders to himself and left them futilely trying to tackle him. On a play against Duke in 1960, using his head, shoulders, and a quick change of pace, he faked an end inside, then ran around his blocker and almost into the arms of a linebacker. He threw a head-and-shoulders fake at him and ran around him, too, to find a defensive back in his path. Using his third fake on the play, he skipped past the back before being knocked out of bounds because he had run out of room on the field to dodge more tacklers.

His biggest problem during the early part of his career wasn't coping with opposing defenses but coping with football pants and stockings that, because of his massive calves, were not wide enough at the knee openings. Consequently, his calves, ankles, and feet were cut off from a sufficient blood flow, and he often suffered severe cramps that cost him playing time.

The problem was finally solved in the opening game of the 1959 season at Boston College. After he scored a touchdown on a twisting 60-yard run, he crumpled to the ground in the end zone. Trainers from both teams rushed on the field and found Bellino writhing in pain from his calves and feet. They removed his shoes and saw that his feet were almost purple. Boston College's trainer, Frank Jones, who had been at the job for nearly four decades, knew immediately that the blood flow to his calves and feet was being constricted by the tightness of his pants and stockings. Red Romo, Navy's trainer, quickly cut the openings and made them wider. End of problem.

But partly because of such miseries and some other leg injuries, Bellino averaged just 11 carries a game during his three seasons at Navy, a low number for someone with his talent. What a healthy Bellino could do was clearly evident against Army in 1959 when he carried the ball 25 times for 113 yards and scored a record-tying three touchdowns.

It was obvious from the start of the 1960 season that Bellino was the special player that everyone expected. His performance against Army at the end of the 1959 season was the hallmark by which he was to be measured, and he lived up to every bit of it. Hardin allowed Bellino to blossom as a senior. In game after game that season, he rolled up a significant amount of yards, though he exceeded 20 rushing attempts in only four games. Still, he finished the year with 834 yards in 168 rushing attempts.

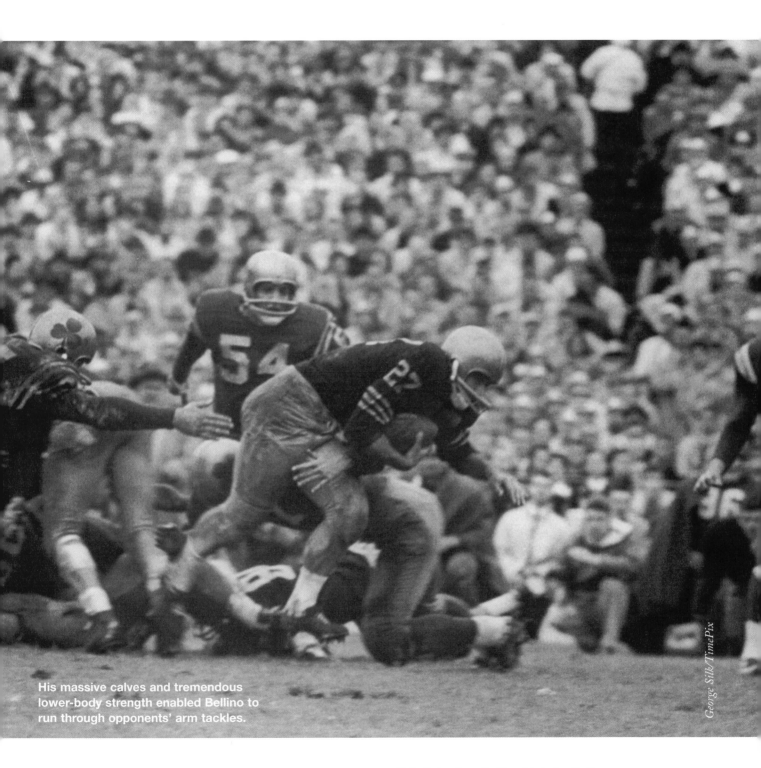

His massive calves and tremendous lower-body strength enabled Bellino to run through opponents' arm tackles.

George Silk/TimePix

Soon, the old salts around the Yard at the Naval Academy were starting to compare him favorably with Buzz Borries, Navy's great running star from 1932 to 1934, who was, until Bellino came along, considered the greatest runner in Navy history.

To be compared with Borries, whom Bellino never met but whose exploits he was well aware of, was the highest praise for any Navy running back. Even nearly 30 years after his playing career had ended, he was considered the epitome of what a Navy running back should be. When the comparison to Bellino began, there were a few raised eyebrows at first, but later everyone agreed that they had no peers up to that time.

The similarities were startling. Slade Cutter, one of Navy's greatest players as an All-American tackle and, like Borries and Bellino, a member of the College Football Hall of Fame, had ample time to compare both men. He played with Borries for three seasons and was athletic director at the Naval Academy during most of Bellino's career. "Buzz Borries was the best running back I ever saw," Cutter said. "Joe Bellino is so close as to hardly make a difference between the two."

Both were superb athletes. Bellino earned six letters in football and baseball and was pursued from high school throughout most of his time at the Naval Academy by major league teams because of his great ability as a catcher. In fact, the Cincinnati Reds offered him a $60,000 bonus to sign a contract with them. Bellino declined because he was determined to become a naval officer.

Borries earned nine varsity letters—three each in football, basketball (his teams were 36–7), and baseball. Cutter once declared that Borries "was the best pass defender we had as a safety, just about our whole pass defense by himself."

The only difference between the two was their physical build—Bellino was built low to the ground with chunky legs that propelled him through tight spaces with the speed and force of a rocket; Borries was lean and lanky and ran with graceful strides but, like Bellino, could change pace and speed in an instant. As a tailback in the single- and double-wing offenses of that time, he was a great passer and a superb defensive back.

Borries also compiled a fabulous combat record during World War II. He served aboard two carriers that were sunk by the Japanese, as executive officer aboard the USS *Lexington* in the battle of the Coral Sea, and then aboard the USS *Gambier Bay* as air officer during the battle of the Philippines Sea. From the latter, Borries managed to launch all of his planes while the vessel was under heavy fire and sinking. After leaving the ship, he took charge of more than 200 men in life rafts for 48 hours until all were rescued.

After he died in 1969, one of Borries' classmates wrote: "Who among us who were so fortunate to see him in action can ever forget the electrifying sight of Buster [his nickname at the Academy among his classmates and friends] Borries under full sail? Certainly not one single opponent. In that flickering instant that it took him to get underway that deceptively awkward-appearing roll of a gait with which he walked was transformed into pure poetry in motion . . . Bustling Buster made daylight with the elusiveness of a shadow, the grace of a gazelle and the power which only an opposing player whose unhappy chore it was to try and impede his progress could evaluate. . . ."

Bellino's achievements at Navy also placed him among a pantheon of great running backs then playing at civilian schools. Joe easily could have joined them because he had more than six dozen full football scholarship offers. But he never wavered in his desire to go to and stay at the Naval Academy, where every moment of his life was accounted for in the routines that train the nation's future naval officers. Playing football was a secondary part of those routines and placed even greater burdens on football players who were forced to cope with the Academy's vigorous academic schedule while trying to accommodate the demands of a football season.

The accommodation didn't work in the spring of his plebe year, and Erdelatz excused him from spring football practice. "Stay out until the fall and put in more study time," his coach told him. "A flunking halfback is no good to me."

Fred Borries.

15

He fully appreciated Erdelatz's decision to lighten his load while he still was acclimating himself to the Academy. "Even as a plebe, I always felt that if it came to a decision of playing football or staying in school, I would drop football," Bellino said. "But I improved my grades and returned to the team in the fall."

Bellino has steadfastly held to his belief that the Naval Academy was the perfect place for his abilities and what he wanted in academics. "As far as football accomplishments are concerned," he noted, "I'm not sure I would have reached those at some place other than Navy. With the ability I had and the type of talent at Navy at that time, I was at the right school, even with all of its demanding routines. In the end, the daily routines and healthy environment helped me be a better athlete. If I had to do it again, I'd still select the Naval Academy."

That was a familiar anthem for nearly every former Navy athlete, particularly football players. It played out just as strongly on the battlefield as it did on the playing field. During World War II, particularly, the roll call of former football players who became war heroes was long and illustrious. The players of the late twenties and thirties commanded the squadrons, submarines, destroyers, and light cruisers as well as the marine rifle companies, battalions, and regiments that led the navy and marines across the Pacific to total victory.

They, in turn, were commanded by Naval Academy players from the century's first two decades . . . like Fleet Admiral William "Bull" Halsey, the nation's most renowned fleet commander during World War II. As commander of the Fifth Fleet in the Pacific, he was known for his bold, aggressive style that epitomized his motto, "Hit hard, hit fast, hit often." As a fullback on the 1902–1903 teams, he led Navy in rushing, and at graduation he was awarded the Thompson Trophy as his class's best athlete. One of only three fleet admirals at the end of the war, he was awarded the Navy Cross, five Distinguished Service Medals, and the Presidential Citation.

Another renowned commander was Admiral John "Babe" Brown, a member of the College Football Hall of Fame for his playing exploits as a lineman and kicker in 1910–1912. During World War II, he was deputy commander of Submarine Force, Pacific Fleet, which helped to cripple Japan's naval and maritime strength by sinking more than 5.7 million tons of shipping. He also was athletic director at the Naval Academy during its football heyday seasons in the early thirties and had several of the great players from those teams as commanders.

One of Brown's teammates was Vice Admiral John Hall, the other guard on the 1911 and 1912 Navy teams. Hall was a genius in landing and supporting American forces in amphibious operations. He did it for General George S. Patton Jr.'s Seventh Army in Sicily in 1943, as naval task force commander in the massive D-Day landings in Normandy in 1944, and for a segment of the invasion of Okinawa in 1945. Lawrence F. Reifsnider, an end on the 1907 team, rose from captain to vice admiral during World War II because of his genius for directing amphibious assaults in Africa and in several Pacific Ocean operations.

Regardless of their football-playing era, competition had taught them to be aggressive and decisive. They understood and stressed the value of teamwork, and

Future Senator John McCain.

17

they had an innate competitiveness that forced them to find a way to win their military battles just as it did to win their football battles. Still, they also fully understood that there might be a supreme price to pay, just as happened to the 13 members of the 1935 Navy team who were killed in action during World War II.

Bellino's class has its own legacy of courage. John Prichard, the team's best wide receiver, was killed in action while serving in Vietnam as a marine captain. Two of his classmates were prisoners of war. Senator John McCain, who languished as a

Slade Cutter.

U. S. Naval Academy Archives

POW in Vietnam after being shot down, was a senior at the Academy when Joe was a plebe. But they knew each other as members of the same company. Bellino just shakes his head when he talks about the horrors that McCain had to endure when he was in captivity. Each shake is worth a thousand words.

As a midshipman, Bellino had to look no further than Cutter, his athletic director, for an example of bravery. Both Cutter and his teammate on the 1932–1934 Navy teams, Robert "Dusty" Dornin, worked under Babe Brown's command as executive officers and skippers of submarines during the first two years of the war and then were given other stateside assignments. So harrowing was the work that no one over 35 years of age could command a boat; nor could any skipper command more than five patrols lest their success in surviving each one begin to give them a feeling of invincibility. Cutter said that's when the absolutely total dedication to every detail that was so vital to survival and success would begin to erode. It was imperceptible at first, but it could mean the difference between survival and loss of the boat and crew.

"I never kept a diary, never took any personal pictures or anything like that because I never figured I'd come back," Cutter once said when describing his job.

Dornin was an end on the 1932–1934 teams, and he played alongside Cutter. They became close friends from their first meeting as midshipmen, but they also had a "friendly" rivalry throughout their navy careers to see who could outdo the other.

Cutter and Lew Parks, another great submarine skipper during the war, returned to Pearl Harbor simultaneously from particularly harrowing patrols and decided to tear apart Honolulu. That was almost a ritual with all submariners on their first night back from a combat patrol as a means of ridding themselves of the life-and-death tensions that had gripped their lives for several weeks. After visiting several bars, they commandeered a jeep that had some guns and ammunition in it and went roaring through the town, shooting at signs, streetlights, and even a huge water tower. The navy's shore patrol (SP) was soon in hot pursuit, and a great car chase ensued. At a fork in the road, they headed to the left to elude their pursuers, but they didn't know the road led directly into the shore patrol's compound. The SPs were waiting for them and immediately detained them.

The next morning, hearing of Cutter's plight, Dornin called the compound and, in his most reassuring voice, said to the officer-in-charge (OIC), "If it would make things easier, I'd certainly be happy to bring down some bread and water so Commander Cutter doesn't go hungry."

"Listen Commander," said the OIC, "I've had it with you guys. You take one step into this area, and I'll throw you in jail, too."

Dornin and Cutter's rivalry included their jobs as executive officers and skippers aboard their submarines, where each vied to see who could sink the most Japanese shipping. Together, they sank more than 300,000 tons and damaged tens of thousands more. Admiral Brown made them verify every sinking or damaged ship they reported, but he never discouraged their rivalry because of the results that it produced. Working in tandem as part of a navy submarine wolf pack, they were at their best because it was like old times on the football field when teamwork was so vital. Together, they were awarded six Navy Crosses, five Silver Stars, three Presidential Unit Citations, two Navy Commendation Medals, and a Bronze Star.

Bellino was only four years old and living in Winchester, Massachusetts, almost within sight of the navy's huge facility in Charlestown, when the Japanese attacked Pearl Harbor on December 7, 1941. The navy had a decided influence in Winchester and was home to many who were stationed there, who worked in the shipyard at the Charlestown Navy Base, or who lived there after retirement,

Robert Dornin.

U. S. Naval Academy Archives

including several admirals and other high-ranking officers. It was that "navy influence" that would later play a major role in his attending the Naval Academy.

Obviously, on that day of infamy in 1941, he was unaware of the attack and its implications. But some five thousand miles away, men who preceded him to Annapolis, and whose legacy as football players he would later share, were in harm's way that day.

William "Killer" Kane, a Navy tackle in the early thirties, was the officer of the day during the attack on Pearl Harbor. He stayed on duty for 48 hours, assisting in caring for the wounded and organizing the survivors. Later during the war, he won two Distinguished Flying Crosses and the Navy Cross. During the battle of Guadalcanal, he successfully crash-landed his plane on the deck of the USS *Enterprise*. He also commanded an air group in Admiral Marc Mitscher's famed Task Force 38/58.

Claude Ricketts played for Navy from 1926 through 1928. He was damage control officer aboard the battleship USS *West Virginia*, which was berthed at Battleship Row when the Japanese attacked. After the ship was struck several times by torpedoes, it appeared ready to capsize. Ricketts, having spent hour after hour preparing in his mind what he would do in such an eventuality, successfully flooded compartments to sink the ship in an upright position. That made it easier to raise and repair the ship, which returned to fight in many naval actions later in the war.

Aboard the USS *Arizona*, Alan Shapley, the starting fullback on Navy's 1926 national championship team, was a marine officer about to be detached from duty aboard the ship. When attack occurred, he was hurriedly given command of an anti-aircraft position atop the battleship's tripod mainmast. When the forward ammunition bunker blew up, dooming the ship, he calmly led his men to the quarterdeck before another explosion blew all of them into the water. He gathered them together and guided them through thick oil, flaming debris, and exploding bombs to nearby Ford's Island, towing an exhausted young marine the last few yards to safety. During the war, Shapley became one of the marines' most decorated officers and later retired as a lieutenant general.

Gordon Paiea Chung-Hoon, a native of Honolulu who starred as a running back on the Navy teams in 1931–1933 and finished his active duty career with the rank of rear admiral, also was aboard the *Arizona* that day, and he also survived. Later in the war, he saved his ship, the destroyer USS *Sigsbee*, after Japanese kamikazes damaged it so badly that it was flooded to the main level. Chung-Hoon managed to keep it afloat so it could be towed to the navy's repair base at Guam.

There were scores of other former players whose bravery and heroism were magnificent. As it was with Dick Antrim, the Medal of Honor also was awarded to Lieutenant Colonel Harold Bauer, a marine aviator who had been a running back on the 1927–1929 teams. But Bauer's award was posthumous.

In 1942, Bauer had led his squadron 600 miles over open ocean to Henderson Field on embattled Guadalcanal. No sooner had he landed than the field was attacked by Japanese bombers. Bauer jumped back into his plane, whose gas tank was just about empty, roared aloft, and shot down one of the attackers. Five days later, he shot down four planes and damaged another, stopping only because he ran out of ammunition. Three weeks later, while circling to land after leading another long over-the-water flight, he raced to the aid of an American destroyer being attacked by Japanese planes. Though again low on fuel, he shot down four of the attackers before crashing into the sea. His body never was recovered, and he is still listed as MIA.

Bellino, as a naval officer, was expected to follow in the footsteps of officers before him when, six months after his June 1961 graduation, he was assigned to the

21

USS *Norfolk* as a deck officer. The ship was a new DL-1 experimental destroyer with a complement of 50 officers and 500 enlisted men. The ship was larger than a conventional destroyer, almost the size of a light cruiser. It had spent nine months being overhauled in the naval shipyard in Norfolk, Virginia, and was dispatched to Guantanamo Bay, in Cuba, for refresher training after the long period of inactivity.

En route, Bellino and his ship ran smack into the Cuban Missile Crisis. The ship's company knew very little about the depth of the crisis or its political and military implications, even after they reached Guantanamo where everything was on a wartime alert status. The *Norfolk*'s job was to guard the entrance to the bay during a huge buildup of men and equipment. After three weeks on such duty, a small boat

delivered two Russian-speaking U.S. naval officers to the *Norfolk*, and it immediately headed out to sea.

"We sailed to the vicinity of Santiago, Cuba, to the west," Bellino recalled, "with orders to intercept a Russian merchant ship allegedly returning missiles to Russia. We found it and saw these tubelike things covered by a canvas, obviously the missiles, stored on their deck. We sailed a parallel course, about 50 yards off the ship's starboard side, with our guns loaded, aimed, and ready to fire, if necessary.

"For a bit, it looked like that would happen because the ship's captain refused to accede to the demands given over a bullhorn by our Russian-speaking officers that they uncover the missiles for our inspection. Though that had been part of the

A group photograph of VMF-212 at Efate Island, New Hebrides, August 20, 1942. Lieutenant Colonel Harold W. Bauer, commanding officer, is standing eighth from the left.

political agreement, the captain wouldn't do anything until he got permission from his superiors. That took about four very tense hours, but we finally achieved the verification."

Bellino recalls his own reactions: "Even though I had graduated from the Naval Academy and was an officer, I didn't feel like I was ready to enter into a battle. But all the senior officers aboard, and especially the 'mustangs'—the warrant officers who had been in the navy for 20 or 25 years and who had fought in World War II and Korea—they were ready for a fight; I mean they really were ready. They said, 'This is it. We've got to do it now.'

"As a young officer, when the skipper says, 'Direct your guns amidship and bear on the merchant ship,' we were ready to fire. It was tense, believe me."

And why not? Bellino's duties included responsibility for the gunnery on the *Norfolk*'s main deck. His guns would fire the first shot.

In November 1963, Bellino left the *Norfolk* and went to minesweeping school in preparation for being assigned as executive officer aboard USS *Albatross* in Sasebo, Japan. The ship was a minesweeper, and the assignment was, in navy parlance, "career enhancing" because of the variety of duties an executive officer is required to perform aboard a small ship. He was the navigator as well as the administrative and personnel officer, really the boss man for the ship's captain, the only officer senior to him on the ship.

The ship was sent to south Vietnam for a three-month mine hunting and minesweeping operation around Camaron Bay, then becoming the navy's biggest logistics and supply port on the Asian mainland. The *Albatross* had to keep the waters around the base clear of any mines that were being sewn by communists in North Vietnam to stymie American supply efforts to help the South Vietnamese army.

It was also believed that a communist guerilla force, soon to be known as the Vietcong, was being supplied for its insurgency campaigns with guns and ammunition from small fishing ships that proliferated in the coastal waters. To check this, Operation Market Time was instituted and the *Albatross* was part of an interdiction force that included minesweepers and coastal craft operated by the U.S. Coast Guard. The *Albatross's* mission was not only to clear the area of any mines but also to stop, board, and search any of the small boats that transited its patrol area.

"The incongruous part of this whole matter," Bellino said, "was while all of this wartime effort was taking place, the Camaron Bay area still was a resort area, renowned for its beautiful beaches and used primarily by the French families still living in South Vietnam. Here we were, working in a wartime readiness situation, and on the bay, girls and their families were water skiing and enjoying themselves on vacation. But that all came to a halt in early 1965 when it became apparent a war was about to ensue.

"One day we pulled into a beach site and had a wonderful cookout for the crew. The next day, a navy destroyer did the same thing, and its people were bushwhacked by the Vietcong and several of them were killed. That's when we opened our eyes and knew what we were doing was a deadly business."

Part of that "deadly business" included acting as a supply platform for detachments of navy SEALs that were conducting clandestine operations on the mainland. Bellino's ship would meet a SEALs team about 15 miles offshore, feed its members, replenish their supplies, and provide a rest stop of about six hours before the SEALs sped off again in the Tigercraft boats on another mission. Three days later, the *Albatross* would rendezvous with the team and again provide rest and replenishment.

"When we picked up a team, it usually was pretty beaten up so we knew they had been in on a lot of action," Bellino said. "What it was we could only surmise because they'd be dressed in black, their faces were blackened to maintain their cover, and they never spoke to us."

One day, Bellino overheard one of the SEALs officers speaking and immediately detected a Boston accent.

"I take from your accent you're from the Boston area," he said to the man. "I'm from Winchester."

There was no reply, but Joe pressed on.

"Say, what do you guys do?" he asked.

"You don't want to know," the officer told Bellino.

And that was it.

"I never got his name so I don't know whatever happened to him," Bellino said. "But he and all the rest of those teams obviously were on very secret missions that were very unpleasant because we found out later that the Vietcong weren't getting their supplies from the small fishing boats but they were being moved from town to town through a very intricate series of tunnels. Those navy SEALs would locate the caches of guns and ammunition and destroy them, and inevitably there would be a firefight between them and the Vietcong."

25

That experience was no different from one experienced by Charles Kirkpatrick, a guard on the same 1930 Navy football team that produced Dick Antrim and Gordon Underwood. In actions that Hollywood saw fit to fictionalize countless times in black-and-white war films, Kirkpatrick led an underwater demolition team under cover of darkness and onto the island of Peleliu to photograph and scout invasion beaches. He did the same thing on the island fortress of Yap, as part of Operation Stalemate. There, he and his team battled their way through a furious firefight against the Japanese defenders before reaching the two hidden rubber rafts that carried them back to a waiting submarine.

Kirkpatrick, later superintendent of the Naval Academy during the glory days of Staubach's teams, was one of the navy's most decorated officers during World War II for participating in operations like that. He won three Navy Crosses, the Distinguished Service Medal, the Silver Star, Legion of Merit, and National Commendation Medal, among many.

Bellino's experiences aboard the *Norfolk* and the *Albatross* were personally very satisfying. But they cost him nearly four years at sea and kept him away from his wife and daughter much of the time they lived in Sasebo. They finally returned to New England while he was on his second tour of Vietnam. That and some other factors finally moved him to resign from the navy.

"It wasn't that I disliked the navy—far from it," Bellino recalls. "It was a great experience. I loved the navy. It was a bad time to make a decision, but I didn't feel I had any other choice. My wife had lost a child at birth, and she was pregnant again, with the prospect still uncertain for a successful birth. There were some other serious family health problems. My wife and daughter had returned to New England. I felt I was just too far away from home to keep a handle on things.

"The first four years of my career had primarily been spent at sea. Doing more of that, along with the prospect of bobbing around again in a small ship, wasn't the least bit appealing. Boats which are 115 feet long aren't made for riding out typhoons in the South China Sea with waves 80 feet high for 11 days at a time. I had done that twice so I said to myself, 'What the hell am I doing here?' It was time for me to get out of there. Taking all of that into consideration, particularly my wife's health, it wasn't that tough of a decision."

Still, the navy tried to induce him to stay. He was contacted by some of its key people telling him, in effect, "We don't want you to leave. You're a very good officer. It would mean a lot to the navy if you stayed." He even could have named a billet, or a ship, or even returned to the Academy as a coach.

While he served his four-year active tour, his life was dedicated to the navy. That dedication never waned, and he stayed very active in the naval reserve for some three decades, his performance levels earning him the rank of captain. When he finally ended his navy service, he was commanding officer, Naval Control of Shipping, Boston Detachment. Achieving captain's rank places him among an elite number of Naval Academy graduates, active and reserve, who earn the eagles worn by a captain or who go on to flag rank.

Shortly after leaving active duty, he signed a contract with the Boston Patriots of the American Football League. Many critics, including navy careerists, complained at the time that he was like too many of the Naval Academy's football players who left the service at their first opportunity without giving the navy a bigger return on its educational investment in them.

That certainly was not Joe Bellino. The naysayers didn't know Bellino, nor did they ever explore the depth of his feelings for the navy. He had long before proved his commitment when, in his junior year, he rejected a $60,000 bonus from the Cincinnati Reds and elected to graduate from the Academy. Though the dreams he brought to the Naval Academy of someday commanding a nuclear submarine had disappeared after a training cruise in an old diesel-type boat, his burning ambition to be a naval officer never flickered.

Playing pro football never occurred to him, he said, until after he decided to resign his commission in 1965. He received a telegram from the NFL's Washington Redskins inviting him to come to their training camp. The Redskins had originally drafted him in 1960, and he reckons that someone in Washington who had

With the ability to pass and kick as well as run with the football, Bellino was a true "triple threat."

George Silk/TimePix

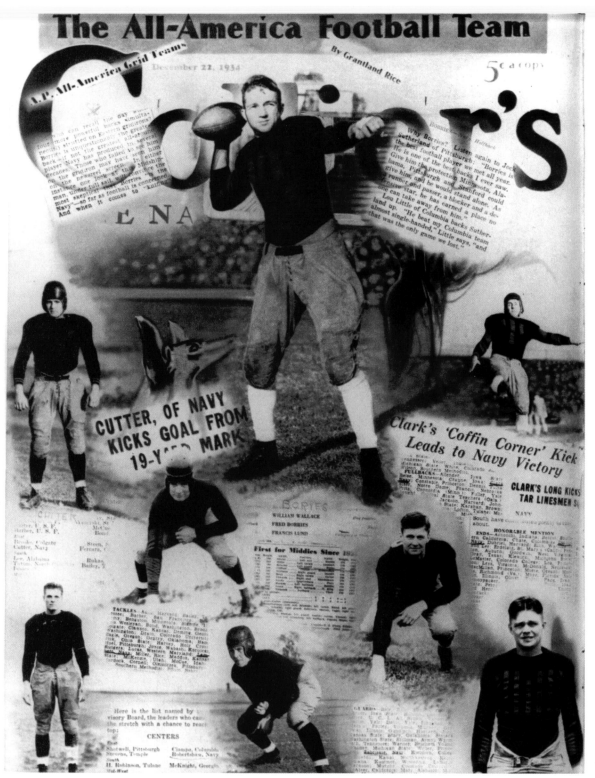

The All-America Football Team

By Grantland Rice

A.P. All-America Grid Teams

December 22, 1934

5¢ a copy

CUTTER, OF NAVY KICKS GOAL FROM 19-YARD MARK

Clark's 'Coffin Corner' Kick Leads to Navy Victory

CLARK'S LONG KICKS TAR LINESMEN S

Navy had a long and distinguished football history even before Bellino became its first Heisman Trophy winner.

processed his resignation papers obviously tipped them off that he was leaving the navy. Soon thereafter, he heard from the Boston Patriots, who also had drafted him for the rival American Football League. At the time, there was a war for talent between the NFL and AFL and fierce competition—with plenty of bucks thrown around—to land high-profile players, such as a Heisman Trophy winner.

During a stopover at Subic Bay in the Philippines, Bellino called the Patriots office in Boston and said he had no other plans after leaving the navy and that he would be interested in playing for them. Unlike Staubach, Navy's other Heisman winner, and later Meyers and McCallum, he never signed a contract until he left active duty. Staubach, Meyers, and McCallum signed with Dallas, Atlanta, and Oakland, respectively, and used their annual leave to attend training camp while still on active duty. McCallum actually played for the Los Angeles Raiders during the regular season while serving aboard a ship based in Long Beach, California.

Bellino has no regrets about the path that he took. "The best four years of my life were in the service," he said. "I had the opportunity to live in Japan with my wife and daughter, before our son was born. I traveled all over the world with the navy."

Who can be surprised at this love affair with the navy? He had been pointed in that direction from birth by his family's doctor, William Barone, in his hometown of Wincheser, Massachusetts. Dr. Barone had delivered him into the world in 1939 and never stopped talking to him about attending the Naval Academy.

"Maybe it was vicarious," Dr. Barone once said about his continual sales pitch. "Perhaps I never got rid of the small-boy appeal Annapolis had for me. Perhaps I took advantage of the friendship I had with the family, but it was my ambition for Joe."

Of course, it wasn't easy. His parents were hardworking, salt-of-the-earth immigrants from Sicily who scrimped and saved to help their family. His father worked in a gelatin plant in Winchester, and Joe had seen his brothers go to work and forego college to help the family sustain itself.

Despite Dr. Barone's constant refrains about the Naval Academy, Joe could also see himself following their path until he started to compete in athletics at Winchester High School. By his senior year, the football scholarship offers became like a blizzard, and his family better understood the necessity for a college education. With the offers at hand, they urged him to pursue college and break away from the limited opportunities he would have by staying and working around Winchester.

No one in that northern suburb of Boston ever was a better athlete. There was little Joe couldn't do on a high school gridiron, and everyone in the state of Massachusetts knew of his exploits. Some were almost of a fictional nature, such as the time he ran 60 yards with 14 seconds to play to get Winchester the state championship. He was all-everything in football, a bona fide major league catching prospect, an all-state basketball guard, and a swimming and diving star.

He was on every college football coach's list, even as a sophomore in high school. Felix "Doc" Blanchard, the 1945 Heisman Trophy winner at Army, came to Winchester High School to recruit a player for West Point. But Joe's high school

29

coach, Henry Knowlton, told him, "You should look at this other kid, this sopho-more we have named Bellino."

"I still remember, as a 15-year-old, going to the coach's office and meeting him and how impressive he looked in his uniform," Bellino recalls. Army, along with Notre Dame and Navy, finally emerged atop his list from the more than six dozen schools that sought him. When Joe overheard Irish coach Terry Brennan tell one of his assistants that he might be too small to play against Notre Dame's opponents, he knocked the school off his list.

When Joe went to West Point for his visit, he was very impressed with coach Red Blaik, but something was missing to turn him on to the school, and his lack of enthusiasm probably was obvious to Blaik, who stopped pursuing him.

"When I visited West Point, I was already leaning toward Annapolis, but what made it worse was going there in the dead of winter," he remembers. "There was an ice storm; the Hudson River was boiling; there were the gray uniforms; the gray buildings; and the gray, overcast skies. That was the impression I was left with.

"Conversely, when I went to the Naval Academy, it was a nice spring day with blue skies; the midshipmen were in their white uniforms; all the girls schools were out visiting; the band was playing; the grass was green; the flowers were in bloom. That stayed with me, too."

Major league baseball teams also courted him with six-figure bonus offers and, despite having been raised in an atmosphere where money always was scarce, he turned them down. His parents didn't play a major role in his decision, feeling it was his to make, but they were overjoyed when he shooed away the scouts and their bonuses and accepted his appointment to the Naval Academy.

When the Cincinnati Reds offered him a $60,000 bonus before his junior year at the Naval Academy, he again agonized about what to do. His four brothers urged him to accept the offer, and again, his parents voiced no opinion, feeling Joe would do the right thing though always hoping that he would stay and graduate. In the end, it was the opportunity to give the navy a try and an obligation to serve that decided the issue.

Navy's assistant athletic director Edward "Rip" Miller used a coterie of scouts nicknamed the "bird dogs," who pursued good football prospects in their home area. In Boston, Edward McCormack and Elliott Rose, two Naval Academy graduates, did the job. They pursued Bellino and his childhood pal Frank Datillo, an end at Winchester High School who later became a very fine player for Navy.

Bellino and Datillo had been close friends since they were toddlers. They decided that their childhood upbringing and other similarities in their families, plus their overall outlooks on life, would be to their advantage if they went to the same school and played football together. Joe always felt the "bird dogs" understood this and that it would be easier to recruit both than just one.

But what had turned them on to the navy—and kept them turned on—were visits that McCormack and Rose had arranged for them to the aircraft carriers USS *Tarawa* and USS *Antietam* when the ships visited the Boston Navy Yard a year apart. Those visits just built upon Bellino's great awareness of things navy in Winchester.

Bellino lacked sufficient credits in math—later his favorite subject at Annapolis—for immediate entry into the Naval Academy and had to attend Columbian Prep, in Washington, D.C., for a year. Columbian, a fine school, was one of the landing spots where prospective Naval Academy entrants spent a year to sharpen their scholastic skills for the academic rigors of Annapolis. Joe didn't mind the extra year in a traditional academic setting because West Point's offer for academic readiness was a summer cram course before plebe year.

While Columbian's academics were first-rate, its football program was so sparse that Bellino's team had just 17 gritty players, including his pal Datillo. The school also was a perennial punching bag for the 62-player Navy plebe team, a rivalry that existed principally so the Annapolis coaches could preview some of the incoming talent. Columbian had never defeated the plebes, but word reached Annapolis in 1956 that it would be different this time.

Bellino put on a great show for the Navy coaches. In the first quarter, he outraced pursuers for a 12-yard touchdown sweep around right end; in the second quarter, he ran 85 yards for a score; and in the third quarter, Datillo's block sprung him on a 32-yard touchdown run. Final score: Columbian Prep, 34; Navy plebes, 33.

One of the very interested spectators that day was Navy's head coach, Eddie Erdelatz, who would soon have Bellino as a player. The next time they met, at the Naval Academy, Eddie personally drove him to the required medical examination. He waited until Joe finished, and as they drove away, Bellino casually told him that he had flunked the examination.

"You what?" exclaimed Erdelatz.

"They said I was overweight," Bellino replied. At the time, Joe was at his playing weight of 187 pounds.

"Come with me," Erdelatz told Bellino, and they went directly to the chief medical officer, a navy captain.

Erdelatz ordered Bellino to take off all his clothes, then asked the doctor, "Is this kid overweight?"

"No," the captain said.

"Well, then give him a waiver," Erdelatz demanded. And he did.

There was little doubt that Joe could play football for the Naval Academy, but under eligibility rules at the time, plebes, or freshmen, were ineligible for varsity competition. With the 1957 plebe team, Bellino became the talk of the Yard at the Naval Academy as he averaged more than 11 yards per carry en route to gaining more than 1,100 yards. He scored 10 touchdowns and moved Commander John "Bo" Coppedge, the plebe coach and himself a former lineman on Navy's great teams of the mid-forties, to describe him as "the finest football player Navy ever had."

When Erdelatz matched the plebes against the junior varsity, Bellino scored both touchdowns for his team, one on an 85-yard run through the middle of the defense.

Even though he only weighed 180 pounds, Bellino's quickness and strength made him a feared running back.

Eredeltz's varsity badly needed a breakaway runner, and after Bellino's performance, Cutter complained, "We've only got one man around here who can go all the way, and it's our luck he's playing for the plebes."

Erdelatz was a very structured coach and a strict disciplinarian. His way was the only way. He stuck by the game plan because he always said every play was drawn to become a touchdown if every player did his job. He wanted no deviations.

After Joe's plebe season, Erdelatz called Bellino into his office and drew a play on the blackboard.

"Joe, this is 27-F, the No. 2, or left halfback, into the No. 7 hole," Erdelatz explained. "The left halfback takes three steps to the right, plants his right foot, and hits that hole."

He then pointed at Bellino and said, "You gotta do what the play says."

Bellino says that Erdelatz knew that if the hole wasn't there, he'd bounce to the outside and maybe run 80 yards for a touchdown.

"I can't have you doing that," he told him.

"When we hit a hole, all three left halfbacks had to do it the same way," Bellino remembers. "It was in, out, and up—into the hole, out of it, and up the field. No deviations. Consequently, Erdelatz never used any of my special talents as a runner, though I did very well as a sophomore until I hurt myself. He had good players, but it was single-platoon football then, and I guess he felt if he had 16 good ones, they could play all the time and win a lot of games."

33

Erdelatz resigned after the 1958 season and Wayne Hardin, his successor, was different. "If you ask coaches who were around us at that time, they would say that Wayne was the best offensive mind ever at the Naval Academy," Bellino maintains. "He gave more leeway to how his backs played. He featured the talent he had. I was a runner so I went inside and outside; I could throw the ball; I could catch the ball; I could quick kick. That's the way he looked at me.

"During the season, he met with me every Sunday afternoon to see how I was feeling and to tell me what special plays he was installing for me for the next game, then he'd tell me he was putting in a couple of plays for me that week. He'd move me around, depending on the play and what we wanted to do. Maybe I'd be fullback, or right halfback, or put at different spots in the backfield. I am particularly grateful that Wayne considered me a special type of back who could handle different plays."

One of Bellino's coaches during his three varsity seasons was Phil Monahan, captain of Navy's famed Team Named Desire in 1954. Monahan suffered a string of knee injuries, and his playing time in his senior season was limited to about 30 minutes. "He gave us 30 minutes of playing time, but he gave us 100 years of leadership," Erdelatz later said. That leadership touched everyone who ever came in contact with him, including Bellino. There was something about him that was special, that forced you to pay attention when he spoke or made a coaching point," Joe remembers.

Monahan was also a superb leader of fighting men. During two combat tours in Vietnam, he twice was awarded the Bronze Star with Combat "V," the Meritorious Service Medal, the Combat Action Ribbon, and the Republic of

Vietnam Cross of Gallantry with Silver Star. He later became a major general in the Marine Corps—you know he had to be something special because the marines don't have many generals—and commanding general of Marine Expeditionary Force/First Marine Division and commander of the giant Marine Corps base at Camp Pendleton, California.

Of course, it was the same with John Hopkins, an All-American tackle who was Monahan's successor as Navy's 1955 team captain. He also became a marine major general and served as deputy commanding general of the First Marine Expeditionary Force in Operation Desert Storm.

During one of his tours in Vietnam, Hopkins was a senior adviser to a South Vietnamese marine unit that was ambushed by the North Vietnamese army. Hopkins had sent his radioman back to the command post and donned the backpack unit himself to direct air support operations and help the marines to escape the trap. This was a delicate assignment because the North Vietnamese always shadowed their opponents, making air and artillery support a dicey proposition with such little separation between forces.

When mortar rounds began falling near his position, potentially closing off an escape route, Hopkins directed a navy A-4 bomber, carrying napalm tanks on its wings, to attack the enemy. The plane screamed toward Hopkins, releasing the canisters and their fiery load and turning the target area around his position into an inferno.

Tom Campbell, another U.S. marine officer who was a member of Hopkins' advisory unit and stationed nearby, frantically called him on his radio. "Leatherneck Two—Two Alpha. How do you read? Over," Campbell yelled into his handset.

"I read you just fine, Tommy," said Hopkins as he walked up and sat down next to Campbell. "Hey! How about a cigarette for a real combat veteran?"

Miraculously, Hopkins survived and walked away, though the handset on his radio was shot in half and two bullets were lodged in his backpack. Had he not been wearing the backpack, the bullets would have killed him.

Bellino's football story, though on a far different plane, has the same characteristics that Monahan and Hopkins displayed in their heroic battle experiences. He demonstrated sheer perseverance coupled with supreme athletic talent wrapped around an unbelievable determination to excel and topped by great personal pride in trying to be the best.

As a player, Bellino continually amazed the millions who watched him play football during his three years at Navy. What they primarily saw was his athletic talent. But those who coached him and played with him and against him got the full panoramic view of a player, and a person, who never settled for anything but being No. 1.

Sometimes he did it by the book; sometimes he didn't, such as in a 1959 game against Maryland, with the score tied and six minutes remaining to be played. The Terps punted the ball to Bellino at the Mids' 41-yard line, and as he started down the field, he was immediately hemmed into the sideline by a wall of potential tacklers.

He could hear Hardin screaming, "Run out of bounds! Run out of bounds!"

In Hardin's eyes, there was no possibility for a long punt return, and he wanted a clock stoppage so he could send quarterback Joe Tranchini back into the game without being penalized, as dictated by the substitution rules at the time. But Bellino deliberately ignored his coach's pleas and suddenly burst toward the middle of the field, sped into the clear, and completed the touchdown run.

"Sure, I heard coach Hardin yelling," he recalled. "But I thought I could find daylight and score and then we wouldn't need a quarterback, except to hold for the extra point."

Hardin was apoplectic one moment and totally forgiving the next when he saw Bellino cross the goal line. "When I saw him going all the way on that play, I suddenly remembered that his high school coach had told me that Joe once told him that when he starts running, he just doesn't know which way he's going to go," Hardin said later.

Someone once asked Hardin whom Bellino reminded him of among the great backs of the past.

"He has the power of Blanchard and the finesse of Davis," Hardin said in his familiar offhanded manner. "But why not just say he reminds me of Joe Bellino. I've never seen another one like him."

35

Despite Bellino's later reminiscences about the way he was not used in Erdelatz's football plans, Eddie had been equally impressed, but he didn't want his young phenom to know it. So, he listed Joe as No. 7 among the left halfbacks when preseason practices began in 1958. But Eddie had already told intimates, "Ordinarily I don't count on sophomores, but I'm counting on this one." After a week's practice, Bellino was at the top of the charts and Erdelatz was ready to make him Navy's featured back. But in the opening game against William & Mary, Joe twisted his knee and never fully recovered for the rest of the season, "because I couldn't cut on that knee, and if I couldn't cut, my game was gone," he said. He gave just a teasing glimpse of his great talent that year against Notre Dame when he roared 82 yards for a touchdown in the first quarter, and in the third quarter, he caught a 46-yard touchdown pass from quarterback Joe Tranchini. The Mids lost 40–20, but the Navy fans had seen the future, and it was spelled Bellino.

In the 1958 Army-Navy game, two Heisman Trophy winners—Dawkins who won the award that year, and Bellino, the 1960 winner—were the touted stars. On a brilliant, sunny, but bitter-cold afternoon at massive Municipal Stadium in Philadelphia, Bellino got the first jump after Dawkins fumbled and lost the opening kickoff. A few plays later, Joe blasted into the end zone for a touchdown, and Navy led 6–0. That and the extra point was all Navy scored that day, stopped by Army's disciplined defense holding Bellino to 45 yards on 14 carries. He added another 40 on pass receptions, but the undefeated Cadets, relying more on running back Bob Anderson than Dawkins, won the game, 22–7.

In 1959, Navy opened the season at Boston College, and it was a huge homecoming for Bellino. Winchester High School moved its scheduled football game to

Navy fans had seen the future and it was
spelled B-E-L-L-I-N-O.

George Silk/TimePix

the morning so that some six hundred of its citizens could go to Boston College and watch their favorite son. He put on a great show that day, but throughout the season Hardin was still wary of his leg problems and treated him like fine, breakable china. Hardin seemed to carefully expose Bellino, all the while working to keep him in shape for the Army-Navy game. Three days before the game, Hardin told him sternly, "I want 60 minutes from you on Saturday."

It was like giving a kid the keys to the candy store.

"It really was like a dream come true because ever since I was in high school and wanting to attend the Naval Academy, I always hoped that a Navy coach would come up and let me play 60 minutes against Army," he recalls. "When coach Hardin said it, it sounded like an order, and to me that meant do it, or else."

As the game approached, Bellino got so excited about his role that he dreamt that he got the ball on a handoff and cut around Army back Bob Anderson. "Even in my dream, I knew I could outrun him," Bellino said. "In the game, that's what I did, but I also had to outrun Joe Caldwell, another back, and that wasn't in the dream. But it came out alright."

It certainly did because Bellino ran 13 yards for Navy's first score and soon found the cracks and openings he needed to slice and dice the Cadets and score two more to become the first Navy player in the modern era to score three touchdowns in one game. He could have made it four had it not been for a series of events that seemed concocted on a Hollywood movie lot.

"Late in the game," he recalled, "we had the ball on the 1-yard line and I called a run for Joe that would have scored," quarterback Joe Tranchini recalled. "But that play never got off because Army jumped offside. We huddled again, and I called the same play. This time, Joe said, 'I've had my big day. How about giving it to Ronnie [Brandquist]. He hasn't scored yet.' Now, Joe was well aware that before his third touchdown, Ronnie had carried the ball four straight times to put it on the 1-yard line where it was easy for Joe to get it across. It was just his way of repaying Ron for doing hard work on his behalf. So I said, 'Sure,' and Ron got the ball and a touchdown against Army."

Bellino did the same thing the following year against Air Force after scoring three first-half touchdowns. In the second half, quarterback Hal Spooner called a play for him at the 2-yard line. "Hold it, Hal," he said in the huddle. "I've got three. Let Joe [Matalavage] get one." So the Navy team captain scored on the next play en route to a 35–3 Navy victory.

This was pure Bellino, not a trumped-up, self-congratulatory exercise to impress his teammates. He had a great feel for people. After a game, he stopped on the street to shake hands with kids who recognized him, and he signed autographs until everyone was satisfied. He once introduced his brother Sam, who was a garage mechanic, to an admiral.

"He made me feel as if I were the admiral," his brother later told friends.

A Washington newspaper ran a weekly football score–guessing contest during the 1960 season, and an eight-year-old boy won one of the weekly contests. When the newspaper interviewed the lad, he said he was a Navy fan and that someday he hoped to play halfback for the Mids like Bellino. Joe called the kid on the phone and invited him and his family to attend Navy's next home game as his guest.

His gregariousness and friendly nature even got him notoriety that he never sought with his famed "bets" with two Naval Academy barbers before the 1960 game against Air Force. To this day, Bellino believes the entire incident was blown too far out of proportion, but it still made a cute story at the time. And whether he realized it or not, it also portrayed him as an ordinary guy.

"I walked into one of the barber shops in Bancroft Hall," he recalled, "and sat down in the chair. 'How much you gonna beat the Air Force by?' Freddie Fernandez, one of the barbers, asked me. 'Oh, 30 points,' I told him. 'You got a bet, he says.'

"I didn't want to bet him, but he kept insisting. So we bet a haircut. If we didn't win by 30 points, he was going to shave my head. If we did, then I'd cut his hair, and he was very bushy on top. Then the other barber, Leon Ross, asked me how many touchdowns I was going to score. 'About three,' I told him, just picking a number from the air. 'You got a bet,' he said. What could I do?"

Navy won the game 35–3 and Bellino scored three touchdowns, so he won both bets. By then, everyone in the country knew of the wagers, so when it came time to pay off, Bellino and the barbers sat down before the entire brigade plus a small army of photographers and television cameras. Joe trimmed a few inches of Fernandez's ample head of hair and clipped off half of Ross' 35-year-old mustache. "I didn't really want to do it, but it had become so big an issue that even the barbers insisted," he said.

Two weeks later, with a game against Duke upcoming, Bellino got a letter from a fraternity at the school, offering to bet several shaved heads that he wouldn't score a point. The students sent a copy of the letter to the *Washington Post* and some other newspapers, hoping it would be a big deal. But Joe didn't bite.

"I wrote them back," he recalled, "and said I wouldn't bet. I told them I was going to be used as a decoy in our offense and wouldn't run the ball more than three times.

"Then I added a P.S. to the letter. 'I would appreciate if you would keep the enclosed a secret until after the game.'"

Ironically, Duke handed Navy its only loss, 19–10 and while he rushed for 62 yards, he was held scoreless for the only time that season.

In 1959 after Navy's 43–12 upset of favored Army, Bellino's 113-yard performance made a prophet of Army coach Dale Hall, who had said a year earlier that he "has the potential to be the best runner in America." It also made believers of the 102,000 spectators who sat awestruck while watching his performance in Philadelphia. Equally convinced were a national television audience and a small army of sports pundits who made Bellino a poster boy for the 1960 season—a Heisman season, as it turned out.

So many of his games during 1960 were memorable because of the seemingly impossible feats that he achieved. During a 41–6 rout of Virginia, he started to run outside right tackle but was suddenly surrounded by six defenders. He later recalled, "All I could see were white jerseys, and I figured, 'I'd better get out of there.'" Guard John Hewitt knocked down one defender; Bellino squirmed out of the arms of another and cut sharply to his left. He quickly shook off a couple more tacklers and moved behind a blocker coming up the left side of the field and along the sidelines. "After that," said Joe, "it was all the way Suzie" . . . all the way to a 90-yard touchdown.

One of his most notable performances, one that put him out front in the Heisman race, came early in the season when Navy defeated third-ranked

Bellino led Navy to a stunning 43–12 victory over Army in 1959.

Washington in a nationally televised game. It allowed everyone in the country to see him perform against top-flight competition. The Huskies were a two-touchdown favorite and had a 7–0 lead before Bellino took over. He returned the kickoff following Washington's touchdown 29 yards, completed a 20-yard option pass, reeled off 17 yards on two consecutive runs, and five plays later dove 1 yard into the end zone for Navy's first touchdown. With less than two and a half minutes to play in the game and his team trailing 14–12, Bellino's running set up Greg Mather's game-winning 41-yard field goal.

After that game, Bellino had no greater fan than Washington coach Jim Owens, who said, "He makes you look like you don't practice tackling much."

When the players' buses rolled into the Yard at the Academy well after midnight, the entire brigade of 3,800 midshipmen turned out to welcome them. They still were hoarse from cheering their team over a special line that had piped their support into Huskies Stadium in Seattle, but the hoarseness didn't show by the gusto in their welcome.

One after another, the players who had starred as well as high-ranking Academy officials were called on to say a few words. When it was Bellino's turn, he walked up to the microphone, looked at his watch, and said: "Holy cow! Do you guys know what time it is?" The resultant howl sent everyone happily to bed.

It was after that game that Bellino became the front-runner for the Heisman Trophy, and his status just increased after a string of fine performances in victories over Air Force, SMU, and Notre Dame. He also had plenty of national television exposure to solidify his Heisman credentials, and he used each game as his own bit of theater to lead up to a thunderous grand finale in a 17–12 victory over Army that nailed down the Heisman Trophy. His touchdown in the game's early minutes helped Navy to a 17–0 lead at halftime. Army came roaring back and with 10 minutes to play in the game trailed just 17–12.

Then, everything came apart for Bellino and Navy. Joe and quarterback Hal Spooner botched a handoff, and Army recovered the ball at Navy's 17-yard line with five and a half minutes remaining. The Cadets moved to a first down at the 6-yard line, but the Mids defense, helped by an errant lateral pass by Army, squashed the scoring threat. Army got one final chance to score on the game's final play when quarterback Tom Blanda heaved a desperate pass into Navy's end zone. Three defenders smothered Army's receiver, and the ball flew into Bellino's hands. He zigged and zagged his way down the field for nearly 45 yards before he was tackled. "That one play may have nailed down the Heisman Trophy," he said.

He was notified by telegram of his Heisman Trophy selection, but the wire was sent to the Academy superintendent, Rear Admiral John F. Davidson. Bellino was summoned to his office from an electrical engineering class. "Usually when you're called to the supe's office, it's because of a disciplinary matter," Bellino recalled. "I couldn't think of any problems. So, my first reaction when he read me the telegram was, 'Thanks a lot, I'm glad I'm not in any trouble.'"

Bellino with the Heisman
Trophy; famed TV personality
Ed Sullivan at left.

Downtown Athletic Club

At a 1977 Navy game, Bellino is honored by Vice Admiral Kinnaird McKee, superintendent of the Naval Academy, for his induction into the College Football Hall of Fame. At right is Executive Director Jimmie McDowell.

Later, during a media interview, he was asked if there was anything in his life that could top it. He paused a moment and said: "You know another fellow from Massachusetts did pretty well this year too: president-elect Kennedy. It might be nice to get a chance to meet him," Bellino answered. The next day, he received a telegram from Kennedy. It read: "Be ready on Saturday. We're sending a limousine to pick you up. Jack Kennedy."

So, he went from hero to legend for all time because a week later at the Downtown Athletic Club in New York City, he received his Heisman Trophy. He later became the first Navy player to have his jersey number retired. Staubach and McCallum were similarly honored.

More than four decades after winning the Heisman Trophy, the award is even more special to him than it was that night in New York when he received it. It was his greatest achievement in athletics, Bellino has always maintained. He still cherishes the day he brought the trophy home to Winchester, accompanied by scores of happy citizens who had gone to the airport to meet him in their own motorcade.

"When a player wins it, it is his family, more than him, who really enjoys the moment," he said. "I had to go back to the Academy to take exams and get ready to play in the Orange Bowl. But it was a bigger joy for my family, for my father who had come over from the old country, for my brother and his family and Dr. Barone and my high school coach. So the joy for me was seeing their reaction, and that reaction has always stayed with me. Sure, I won it, but in reflection, it really was what it meant to the Naval Academy and to my family and friends."

Today, the trophy sits in the den area of his home. Until his mother died a number of years ago, it was at her home almost as a tribute to the support his family had given him. When his children were growing up, he often used it as an example of an achievement for which so much work and effort was required.

That effort will be forever recognized by the trophy that says he was the best at what he did on the playing field for one season. But it also represents the collective efforts of his teammates who worked so hard to make it possible and who willingly toiled and sacrificed whatever was necessary to make their team and him achieve personal glory.

43

Thus, it was apt and fitting that six months after his graduation from Annapolis, Bellino also was chosen to make the traditional presentation of his class's yearbook, *Lucky Bag*, to the president of the United States, John F. Kennedy. Joe, then an ensign about to embark on his first sea duty, represented more than 700 other young ensigns who had chosen to serve their country, even to the point of paying the ultimate price. The recipient of the book was himself a navy war hero who had nearly paid that price in battle and during his subsequent heroic efforts to rescue the crew of his doomed PT boat during World War II.

Together, they shared a spirit known only to them and to others like them who willingly accept the ultimate service.

Chapter 2

Doc Blanchard and Glenn Davis

Blanchard and Davis.

Without question, they are the greatest backfield tandem in college football history. No first names, please, because a half-century before Michael Jordan and Tiger Woods became simply Michael and Tiger, Blanchard and Davis achieved a status where everyone knew who they were and what they did.

But for the record, Felix Anthony "Doc" Blanchard and Glenn Woodward "Junior" Davis burst like a fiery meteor upon college football's scene in 1944 as members of the same West Point backfield and spent three seasons performing some of the most amazing feats ever seen on a college gridiron.

Thus, it is impossible to separate them because nearly six decades after they played their final game at West Point, no duo has even come close to displacing them, and it is highly unlikely that one ever will. (They can be seen on the opposite page, Davis (no. 41) carrying the ball with Blanchard (No. 35) nearby.)

At West Point from 1944 to 1946, Blanchard and Davis never played in a losing game while their teams posted a 27–0–1 record. They were the integral part of an Army football dynasty that won national championships in each of their three seasons. Individually, they each won every major award given to college football players, including the Heisman Trophy. They were the only Heisman winners ever to play in the same backfield together.

In 1959 and 1961, respectively, Blanchard and Davis were inducted into the College Football Hall of Fame, though to the dismay of their former coach at West Point, Earl "Red" Blaik, they entered in separate years.

"There is no reason why they could not have gone in together," Blaik said at the time. "All that they ever achieved on the playing field, they did together."

Blaik always insisted that Blanchard and Davis be linked as one. He once refused to allow Pete Martin, the top writer for the *Saturday Evening Post*, then the nation's most popular weekly magazine, to interview Blanchard by himself.

"I never separate them," Blaik told Martin. "If you want to write a story on both, I'll cooperate. But if you want to do a story on just one of them, you won't get any cooperation from me, and you sure won't get any from them if they know I'm not for it."

Martin wouldn't budge and went home without his story. But when Army went to New York City the following week to play a game, there he stood, awaiting the Army team's arrival and more than willing to write about both players.

On the football field, they presented the perfect combination of speed, power, and athletic excellence that were unmatched at any school, ever. Thanks to George Trevor, a sportswriter for the *New York Sun*, Blanchard, a 6', 210-pound fullback, became known as Mr. Inside; and Davis, a 5'9", 170-pound halfback with world-class speed, was called Mr. Outside. There were many occasions, however, when those titles were perfectly interchangeable, as every one of their opponents regretfully found out.

They and their teams were reflections of what West Point football was all about. Though the Blanchard and Davis teams were rich in talent beyond all imagination—at least a dozen All-America players were teammates—they were always motivated to play all out. "That was the nature of the place," said Blanchard. "There's not much there to distract you. When we played there was no outside media, so we did what we had to do and got along OK. Everyone was motivated to do what was best for the team. And if we ever wanted to do differently, then Colonel Blaik very quickly got us back on track."

Both are proud of the fact that they played on both offense and defense for their entire careers. They did so with such distinction that they could have gone into the Hall of Fame as either offensive or defensive players.

"Glenn would get off a 40-yard run, and before he could catch his breath, he would be blocking for me, or playing safety on defense," Blanchard said.

"Having to play for so long at a stretch really kept our heads in the game," Davis said. "We had to concentrate all the time, and that helped to make us better players."

Their career statistics are a great insight into just what they accomplished, though Blanchard once said, "Nobody paid any attention to statistics when we

46

One of the most famous football games in history was played in Yankee Stadium in front of 74,000 fans on November 9, 1946. Army, undefeated and ranked number one, faced undefeated number two–ranked Notre Dame. There were four Heisman Trophy winners on the field (Davis and Blanchard from Army, and Leon Hart and Johnny Lujack from Notre Dame), and one Outland Trophy winner (George Connor of Notre Dame). The game ended in a 0–0 tie.

Downtown Athletic Club

Courtesy of Westpoint

President Harry Truman greets captains Dan Foldberg, left, and Tom Bakke before the 1950 Army-Navy game. Navy pulled off a huge upset, winning 14–2 and ending an Army winning streak dating back to 1947.

Nearly six decades after his graduation from West Point, Glenn Davis is still considered by many to be the best athlete ever to have attended the school.

48

Downtown Athletic Club

played. I don't remember any reference to how many yards or how many touchdowns each of us made."

Davis concurred. "Doc and I each would perhaps handle the ball about 15 times a game on offense, counting runs and passes, which wasn't very much compared to what running backs did even 10 years after we played, and which has grown a lot since then," he said. "But he [Blanchard] also was blocking, tackling on defense, punting, and kicking off."

Still, just how dynamic they were together can be gleaned from their combined career records: 97 touchdowns and 585 points—still an all-time record for a starting backfield—and 4,623 rushing yards. Davis scored 59 touchdowns, and 43 of those were from rushing; he caught 14 touchdown passes, and scored on two punt returns. He also threw five touchdown passes—all to Blanchard. Doc also had 26 rushing touchdowns, four from pass interceptions and one on a 92-yard kickoff return.

They had two great common assets: athleticism and speed. Nearly six decades after he graduated, Davis still is considered the greatest athlete in West Point history. He established an Academy record in his physical efficiency test with $926^{1}/_{2}$ points (out of a possible 1,000). During his career there, he won 11 varsity letters in football, basketball, baseball, and track.

As a baseball player, he consistently batted around .340 and averaged a stolen base per game. While facing future major league pitcher Hal Gregg in an exhibition game against the Brooklyn Dodgers' Montreal farm club, he was three-for-five, and in one inning he beat out a bunt, then stole second, third, and home. No wonder Dodgers president Branch Rickey later told him, "I'll hand you a blank Dodgers contract. You can fill out whatever amount is fair." Rickey later estimated his value at $75,000, a princely sum back then.

In track, he was a world-class sprinter who set a Military Academy record of 9.7 seconds in the 100-yard dash and 20.9 in the 220-yard dash. He did so after playing a four-hour baseball game against Navy, then jumping into a car for the trip to the track meet, all the while changing his track uniform as the car sped along. He wore a borrowed pair of track shoes and set both records without much of a warm-up. He even was considered a solid choice to make the 1948 Olympic team until his Army career and an injured knee prevented him from taking an active part in the tryouts.

49

Said Colonel Don Hull, on the U.S. Military Academy's physical education staff at the time and later head of the United States Olympic Committee: "Most of us on the PE staff felt that Glenn was the greatest athlete ever produced in America, to that point. Some of us believed that had Davis been a track man and not a football player, he and not Bob Mathias might have won the 1948 Olympic decathlon gold medal."

In response to a query after *Time* magazine once favorably compared Davis' athletic gifts to those of Jim Thorpe, Blaik said: "You take Thorpe. I'll take Davis. In a half century of college football, I've seen some great players. None were better than Glenn Davis."

Then, when asked about the great fullbacks of college football's first half century of its modern era, he said, "You take [Bronko] Nagurski, I'll take Blanchard."

Blanchard was no slouch as an athlete. He ran 100 yards in 10 seconds, sometimes faster. Looking for something to help him stay in shape during the off-season, he joined Army's track team as a shot-putter. In high school, he had dabbled with it but could attain only about 30 feet. Two months after taking it up at West Point, thanks, ironically, to help from teammate Ralph Davis, Glenn's twin brother, he won the IC4A Indoor Championships with a heave of 48 feet, 3$^{1}/_{2}$ inches. Later that year, he set a Military Academy record of 51 feet, 10$^{1}/_{2}$ inches.

But it was in football where Blanchard flashed his greatest athletic credentials. He was part of a four-generation football family who had carried the family torch handed to him by his father, "Big Doc" Blanchard. "Big Doc" had been a great 240-pound fullback at Tulane for Clark Shaughnessy in 1915–1916 and 1920. Army's Blanchard had long been nicknamed "Little Doc" because those who had seen him and his father play football said they were almost mirror images of each other in their style. "Little Doc," in turn, handed the torch to his son Tony, a tight end at North Carolina (1968–1970); Tony then passed it to his son, and Doc's grandson, Rhett, who played tight end for Wake Forest during the early nineties.

Doc was no secret when he arrived at West Point in June 1944 because he had been heavily recruited three years earlier by many colleges while attending St. Stanislaus Prep School, near New Orleans. Many believed he would follow his father's footsteps to Tulane University. But "Big Doc" was very ill and was living in South Carolina, so "Little Doc" chose the University of North Carolina.

There he forged a tremendous reputation as a 225-pound freshman fullback. With World War II underway, he tried to join the Navy's V-12 preflight program at North Carolina, but he washed out because of color blindness and his weight. He exceeded the limit by three pounds despite going on what he termed "a big-time diet," and a failed, feverish attempt by his mother's cousin, freshman coach Jim Tatum, to "boil him down" to the prescribed limit. Navy lore says that the doctor who flunked him was later tracked down and transferred to the Aleutian Islands because had Blanchard passed the physical, he surely would have wound up playing football at the Naval Academy instead of being a prime mover in beating Navy during each of his three seasons at West Point.

He then was drafted into the army and served as an enlisted man for nearly a year and a half in the chemical corps while "Big Doc" worked to get him an appointment to West Point. Blaik also was well aware of Blanchard's talent and worked equally hard before securing an appointment from North Carolina Senator "Cotton Ed" Smith. Six weeks before the start of football practice in 1944, he became a member of the Corps of Cadets.

"I could have played at 240–245 pounds, but Colonel Blaik wanted players who could run fast, and he wouldn't tolerate any fat boys. He traded speed for bulk," Blanchard said. "Of course he was correct, as he always was, because I felt much stronger playing at 210 pounds because I could do everything I wanted. I had much more speed and stamina."

Those 210 pounds were spread over his six-foot frame so that his body looked as if it had been sculpted by one of the masters. He was truly a one-man force who, when he ran, was an equal-opportunity destroyer. It didn't matter whether the defenders were bigger, smaller, or just as big as he was. He ran over all of them, and during his career, he left several lying on the ground in a temporary comatose state.

Blanchard as a cadet alongside an All-America trophy.

As a North Carolina freshman, he once ran over a pair of varsity tacklers with such force that they too were knocked out. From that time on, varsity defenders wanted no part of him.

Blaik wrote: "Doc Blanchard was the best-built athlete I ever saw: six feet and 210 pounds at his peak, not a suspicion of fat on him, with slim waist, Atlas shoulders, colossal legs."

At West Point, he played fullback and linebacker, and, as previously noted, he did it so well that he would have made the Hall of Fame at either position had substitution rules limited his playing to either offense or defense. Dick Duden, a

Hall of Fame end for Navy, once said, "Blanchard was one of the best football players I ever saw. In the 1945 Army-Navy game, I remember him for his defense as
much as for his offense because the pass that he intercepted and returned for a
touchdown was intended for me. All I saw was the back of his helmet going the
other way to the end zone."

In the 1946 game against Notre Dame, Blanchard slammed into Irish
All-American running back Emil Sitko so hard that the collision sent Sitko and his
helmet flying in different directions. But to do that, Blanchard had brushed aside a
determined block by Johnny Lujack as if he weren't there.

"Mr. Inside," Doc
Blanchard (No.
35), combined raw
power with speed
and athleticism to
become one of
the most domi-
nant runners in
Army history.

"I enjoyed playing linebacker because that's where all the action was," Blanchard said. "I played behind Tex Coulter and Barney Poole, which made my job so much easier because they were such great players. Tex was somewhat a hatchet man, and I'd just say, 'Sic 'em, Tex,' and step back from time to time and let him do the job. When we played a great Michigan team in 1945, he literally knocked out Len Ford, their best defensive lineman."

Blanchard did more. He punted and consistently kicked off into the end zone, or at least to the goal line. In those rare instances when his kickoffs were returned, he delighted in roaring down the field and usually tackling the ball carrier.

He was a splendid pass receiver, and his unselfish blocking for Davis and the other running backs was an awesome sight. During the 1944 game against Notre Dame, Doug Kenna was returning a punt from sideline to sideline when John "Tree" Adams, Notre Dame's 6'7", 218-pound All-American tackle, running at full speed, had him boxed in and was ready to smother him. Blanchard, also running at full speed, hit Adams with a blind-side block that not only flattened and finished the Notre Dame player for the day but also could be heard over the roar of more than 75,000 spectators at Yankee Stadium.

"He was something to run behind," Davis said. "He'd get into defensive players and he was just like a steamroller. He'd be going at full speed, and with all of that power he generated when he ran, he'd flatten them, put them right on the ground, or drive them so far out of my route that they never had a chance to make a play. I'd get just a glimpse of what he was doing and didn't really have a chance to stick around and admire it. But I always was glad that I wasn't a defensive player trying to take him on. It was no contest, especially for small defensive backs like myself."

His feats reached almost legendary proportions, and many saw him as the real-life embodiment of the popular comic book character Superman.

And maybe he was.

In 1944, after Blanchard helped the Cadets to a rollicking 59–0 victory over his unbeaten Notre Dame team, Irish coach Ed McKeever wired South Bend: "Have just seen Superman in the flesh. He wears No. 35 and his name is Blanchard."

Everything about him was pure physical power. He burst into a hole with a sprinter's speed, running with strong, powerful strides. If there was someone in his way, that defender was a road-kill candidate; if there was a defender nearby, Blanchard simply veered a couple of steps away from him, before setting his course for the end zone. His 10-second speed for the 100-yard dash (players weren't timed in the 40-yard dash at that time) enabled him to run away from any defender he didn't run over.

Early in the 1946 season, Michigan was favored to tame the Blanchard-Davis combination. Blanchard had missed the previous two games with a torn anterior cruciate ligament, a season-ending injury for most players. Yet, he had one of the most stirring individual efforts of his career. He scored two of Army's three touchdowns; in the last one, he carried three defenders for the last five yards for the winning score, proving once more that it really didn't matter whether there was no hole at the line of scrimmage.

Joe Steffy, an All-American guard and winner in 1947 of the second Outland Trophy presented to the nation's best collegiate lineman, had to block for Blanchard for two seasons. There were times, he says, when it wasn't that easy.

"He was a tough runner, really big for those times because he went between 210 and 215 pounds," Steffy said. "He could run inside with the speed of a halfback, and an offensive lineman had better get the block done for him because there were times when he plowed you and the defensive guy right out of the play."

A few days before the 1945 Army-Navy game, Blaik held one final dummy scrimmage (hard blocking but no tackling). Blanchard ran a dive play, and when the hole on the line of scrimmage didn't open properly, he just stomped over his own players, particularly center Herschel "Ug" Fuson.

"Run that one again!" Blaik barked.

Fuson looked up and said, "Colonel, if we run this play much more, you're not going to have any center left."

"For a big man," Blaik said, "Doc was the quickest starter I ever saw, and in the open he ran with the niftiness, as well as the speed, of a great halfback. He was a terrific tackler and blocker. He could catch passes, punt, and kick off exceptionally well. He had great instinctive football sense, supreme confidence, and deep pride. He could have become an Olympic decathlon star if he had been serious about it."

Army's line coach at that time, Herman Hickman, the sage of Tennessee's Ozark Mountains, declared: "This is the only man who runs his own interference."

Blaik once recalled two games against archrival Navy where Blanchard ran head-on through eager tacklers and, without breaking stride, raced to a touchdown.

After Blanchard scored three touchdowns when Army defeated Navy for the national championship in 1944, John McEwan, former Army coach and Hall of Fame center, cracked: "If I were a Navy man and saw Blanchard coming, I'd resign from Annapolis immediately."

Arnold Tucker, Blanchard's quarterback in 1945 and 1946, said he "was an absolutely awesome weapon. No matter what era he played in, he'd still be a star, just as great as when he played for Army because he combined the two great talents of speed and strength."

Jim Enos, a lineman who played for three years with Blanchard, agreed. "If you could take Doc as he was when he played at West Point and put him through the various conditioning and strength programs that athletes go through today, he'd still be awesome. His 6' and 210 pounds might be considered small if you go strictly by numbers. But at 6' and 225 pounds, he'd match any of the current great running backs. Add his speed, strength, and toughness, and there's no doubt that he'd still be a star."

"I'd like to come back as a 240-pound fullback, and I'd be just as fast and strong as I was when I played for Army," Blanchard said with a laugh. "Or maybe I could be a linebacker at that size. Both would be fun."

What was it like to tackle him?

Navy's Hall of Fame center and linebacker Dick Scott, who grew up outside West Point's gate in Highland Falls, New York, and played against Blanchard and Davis in two Army-Navy games, said it was an unforgettable experience, "if you lived through it."

"He came into the line with his head down and his knees churning up a couple of thighs that were as big as giant tank traps," Scott said. "You were really lucky to ever get a good piece of him by yourself because he simply sent tacklers sprawling who tried to take him one-on-one. Added to that was his great speed for the first 10 or 15 yards that got him into and away from the line of scrimmage so quickly that guys were clutching and grabbing at him from behind. If he got into the open, then he was even a more fearsome weapon against linebackers and defensive backs who were smaller than him."

Eight years after he graduated, Blanchard returned to West Point as an assistant coach, and Blaik had him race against the varsity in the short sprints, or gassers, designed to improve the players' swiftness and endurance. He beat an entire squad that was renowned for its speed.

Old-timers at West Point who had seen four decades of Army football to that time often compared him to Paul Bunker. It was the highest possible praise because Bunker epitomized all that an Army football player was about—on and off the gridiron.

Bunker was a four-year letterman from 1899 through 1902 as a lineman and fullback and the earliest West Point football player to be elected to college football's Hall of Fame. He was picked on the exclusive Walter Camp All-America team as a tackle in 1901 and then as a halfback in 1902, one of only two players ever so honored by Camp.

In 1941, at the age of 60 and getting ready to retire after nearly 40 years in the army, he had returned to San Francisco after serving with the 59th Coastal Artillery Battalion on Corregidor in the Philippines. That island fortress guarded Manila Bay, and anyone wishing to use the valued port of Manila had to pass Corregidor.

But with the war clouds getting ever darker in the Pacific, he contacted his good friend, West Point classmate and manager of his 1902 football team, General Douglas MacArthur, commander of army forces in the islands, and volunteered to rejoin the unit. MacArthur enthusiastically accepted his offer and gave him back his old command.

No sooner had he arrived than the Japanese invaded the islands, and he was part of the army's gallant, but ultimately futile, struggle through the first five months of 1942. When President Franklin D. Roosevelt ordered MacArthur to leave the Philippines and go to Australia to command U.S. forces in the southwest Pacific, the first half of his journey from Corregidor to the island of Mindinao was made in navy PT boats. To ensure a safe getaway, Bunker's artillery men let loose a furious barrage of covering fire while the boats sped into the open sea and escaped the Japanese naval blockade.

Blanchard (left) and
Davis in practice.

MacArthur (back row, in military dress) with the 1902 West Point football team.

AP/Wide World Photos

A few weeks later, Corregidor was overrun by a Japanese invasion force, and before it finally capitulated, Bunker hauled down the Stars and Stripes from a flagpole that had somehow survived five months of constant bombing and shelling.

To prevent the Japanese from desecrating the flag, he burned it, but not before cutting out a strip. He then cut the strip in half, sewing his half under a patch on his khaki shirt and giving the other half to Colonel Delbert Ausmus; each agreed that if either died before they were liberated, they would take both halves and deliver them to U.S. forces.

Bunker died 10 months later, in March 1943, of starvation in a Japanese POW camp on Formosa (Taiwan). He was clad in the same uniform—then nothing but rags hanging off his emaciated body—that he had worn at Corregidor and as a prisoner. Lieutenant General Jonathan Wainwright, commander of the American forces in the Philippines at the time of surrender, was at his side when he died.

Ausmus took the strip of flag from Bunker's tattered uniform before he was buried, along with a diary Bunker had been keeping, and hid them from his captors. When he was repatriated in 1945, he presented both strips of flag and the diary to Secretary of War Robert Patterson.

FIELD OF VALOR

While Blanchard exhibited the same brute strength and athleticism that had marked Bunker's Hall of Fame career, Davis was poetry in motion. There wasn't anything he couldn't do on a football field. Yet it is a mistake to think of him as a light, shifty half-back. He ran inside with surprising power, and on his dazzling, broken-field runs, the power in his legs was enough to often burst through the arms of would-be tacklers. Like Blanchard, he could kick and was an excellent passer and pass receiver.

Early in the 1946 season, Tucker injured his shoulder so badly that he could barely raise his arms to shoulder level, and this badly crimped Army's long passing game. So it was thrust on Davis. The ball either was centered through Tucker's legs to Davis, or Tucker took the snap, turned around, and merely flipped the ball to Davis. Either way, Glenn used halfback option passes to reach receivers running downfield. He completed 19 of 47 passes that season, and five of them resulted in touchdowns.

Perhaps one of Davis' most overlooked talents was his blocking ability. While Blanchard was renowned for clearing a path for Davis on some of his end sweeps, Davis was a superb lead blocker for Blanchard's inside running plays. Then there was his defense. During each of his seasons at West Point, his speed, agility, and overall athleticism made him the best defensive back in college football, a distinction that was rarely noted because of his great offensive ability.

"Glenn Davis," Blaik once said, "could do anything you asked him to do and he could do it better than anyone else."

Ironically, Blaik, who had been an assistant coach at West Point back in the late twenties, had also coached West Point's previous great backfield tandem— Christian "Red" Cagle and Harry Wilson. In his book *You Have to Pay the Price*, he ranked Cagle with Blanchard and Davis as "the three greatest backs I ever coached."

"I doubt there was ever a more thrilling back to watch than Red Cagle . . . he ran with speed, power, elusiveness—and great instinct. He was equally dangerous, right or left. As a cutback artist, he was superb. He ran with long strides . . . he was dynamic on the option run or pass. If tacklers threatened to inundate him, he broke away from them in backward diagonals until he could enflank or elude them and turn upfield again."

Blaik very easily could have been talking about Davis.

Davis came to West Point in 1943 after a tremendous athletic career at Bonita High School in LaVerne, California, where he earned 13 letters. In his senior year, he won the Helms Athletic Foundation's trophy as the best schoolboy back in his area by scoring a California-record 236 points and leading undefeated Bonita to the southern California small schools title that season.

Blaik heard about Davis from an old friend, Warner Bentley, a professor of dramatics at Dartmouth College, where he had coached before coming to West Point. The Pacific Coast Conference was in the midst of trying to purify itself at the time and wasn't pursing with great diligence any of California's outstanding high school players. But Glenn's parents eagerly listened to Blaik's proposal that their son could attend West Point. Glenn had just one proviso—that his twin brother Ralph

59

(Glenn was born 10 seconds after Ralph, hence the nickname "Junior") should also go because they had been almost inseparable since birth. Blaik easily found an appointment for Ralph, too.

With World War II in full swing, the eligibility rules then in effect permitted plebes, or freshmen, to play on the football varsity, and Davis immediately became a starter. Blaik had junked his favorite single-wing system and switched to the T formation where Davis became a triple-threat fullback, then a halfback. He scored eight touchdowns and was seventh in the nation in total yardage that season.

All of that was forgotten—and it is rarely referred to when speaking of Davis' career because of his great years teamed with Blanchard—when he was "found," or dismissed, from the Military Academy for failing math grades. No one worked harder to master the subject, to the point where he'd fall asleep over his books after a day of marching, classes, and football practice. His roommate would roll him into bed and set the alarm clock for another prereveille study session. Undaunted by the failure, he returned home, enrolled in a special four-month math course at Pomona College, and was readmitted to West Point in 1944.

"I had to come back because I didn't want to be perceived as a loser," he said. "It meant a great deal to me to graduate. My twin brother Ralph was there, and I wanted to continue playing football for Army. The problem when I came the first time was not being prepared academically for what they demanded. There were teammates who'd been there two or three years, or guys who had come from other colleges, who knew how to handle the academics.

"The time I gave to football that first year also cost me. It was time that I could not devote to staying up with the academics, and I paid the price. It was never easy during the three years after I returned because of the time that athletics took. But I was determined to get through it, no matter what it took."

In another irony, on his train trip east to reenter West Point, he sat next to Clark Shaughnessy, who, as noted earlier, had been the head coach at Tulane when Blanchard's father was the team's fullback. "He told me about a boy who had just entered the Academy and was destined to become a great back," Davis later related. "He told me the boy's name, and I made a point to remember it. It was Felix Blanchard."

"Davis," Steffy said with a voice still filled with awe six decades after playing with him, "was the greatest athlete I ever saw, and that means in any sport because he played most of the major ones at West Point where some of his records still stand.

"As a running back, he made his linemen look great because we never had to flatten anyone to get him room," Steffy said. "All we had to do was to get in the guy's way and Glenn would run off that little shield, though you can bet that Colonel Blaik wasn't tolerating simple shield blocks. We knocked guys down because we had to. But in the open field and on the move, Glenn didn't need a lot of help to keep him going."

"When I'd get a block on a defender to spring him around end," Blanchard said, "he was awesome to watch when he got going. He was also a strong inside

Blanchard (No. 35) played linebacker on defense; many knowledgeable observers feel he would have been an All-America selection even if he had never played a single down on offense.

USMA Library Special Collection and Archives Division

runner for someone who was about 5'9" and 170 pounds. He had great balance to go with his strength and speed. The key to his success really was his speed and quickness because tacklers never got a straight shot at him."

The irony of Davis' talent is that he, like all great running backs with his style, could never describe what he did and how he did it. Like them, he had great field vision and instincts that, like radar, guided him in his journey through opposing defenses. What his eyes saw and his senses felt was somehow transmitted to his feet

Glenn Davis.

Downtown Athletic Club

and legs, then translated almost computerlike into how he moved. "I always had a plan when I started out because that was the play that was called," Davis said. "But I never knew where I was going to wind up because my instincts and my legs, combined with my speed, got me there without me thinking too much about it."

Davis was a world-class sprinter who regularly ran the 100-yard dash in less than 10 seconds. He translated that speed to the football field, and once he broke into the clear, no one could ever recall him being caught from behind. Davis scored 27 touchdowns on plays from 37 to 87 yards. He finished four seasons at West Point with 4,129 total offense yards and was Army's all-time rusher with 2,957 yards, from 358 carries. That record lasted 44 years until Mike Mayweather, who carried the ball 495 more times than Glenn, totaled 4,299 from 1987 through 1990. In 1945, Davis set college football's current all-time single-season record of 11.5 yards per rushing attempt. He had an identical figure to lead Army in 1944, but he was 17 attempts shy of the required 75 to 100 attempts necessary to qualify for the collegiate record. The low number of rushing attempts was a result of the Cadets' powerful two-unit team that built up such huge leads that he played less than half a game each week.

One of the most memorable moments in his football career occurred during the 1945 Army-Navy game when, as a defensive back, he just missed knocking down a pass to Navy back Clyde "Smackover" Scott, a future Olympic silver-medal sprinter.

"Clyde, who was a world-class sprinter, was running his pattern full steam to the end zone," Tucker remembered. "Davis had to stop, change direction, and then go after him. I'll be darned if he didn't catch him within 45 yards. Their momentum carried both of them into the end zone. Navy had a score but Davis' pursuit and speed were the most incredible things I ever saw on a football field."

Tucker said that Davis was so fast off the mark that on dive plays he often had to race down the line of scrimmage to make the handoff. "There were a couple of times when I didn't get there in time and had to keep the ball and run around end," he said. "I know that when we beat Oklahoma in 1946, that so-called keeper play was a key in our victory. Everyone said how great a call it was, but, believe me, it wasn't a great call. I simply did not get the ball to Glenn in time for the handoff, and the Oklahoma defense was so keyed into him, they forgot to protect the outside and I ran free."

Pity the defenses trying to cope with this pair. When they tried to stop Blanchard by packing their defenses from tackle to tackle, Davis was turned loose to the outside. The alternative wasn't very good, either—spread out and try to keep Glenn from getting outside, thus opening some natural holes in the middle of the defense for Blanchard, who was fast enough to turn off-tackle plays to the outside and into big gainers and who was an awesome weapon for some 165-pound defensive back to take on.

In his book *You Have to Pay the Price* Blaik wrote: "Anybody who ever saw Davis carry the football, must realize there could not have been a greater, more dangerous running back in the history of the game. He was emphatically the greatest halfback I ever knew. He was not so much a dodger and a side-stepper as a blazing runner who had a fourth, even fifth gear in reserve, could change direction at top speed, and fly away from tacklers as if jet-propelled."

Thus was born the rhyme: "Ashes to ashes, dust to dust./ If Blanchard don't get you, then Davis must."

Though they are forever linked, everything about Blanchard and Davis was different, except their desire to excel on the football field. "We were casual friends,"

In 1946 Davis and Blanchard electrified a war-weary nation just beginning to turn its attention to other pursuits. The 1945 Army team is believed by many to be one of the best college teams ever.

TIME
THE WEEKLY NEWSMAGAZINE

JUNIOR DAVIS & DOC BLANCHARD
They make Army's T boil.
(Sport)

Time Pix

Blanchard says of his West Point relationship with Davis. "We were placed in companies by height and were in different regiments. I saw him mainly at meals and during football season, at practice. I knew his brother Ralph better because we both were shot-putters on the track team while Glenn mainly played basketball in the winter and baseball in the spring."

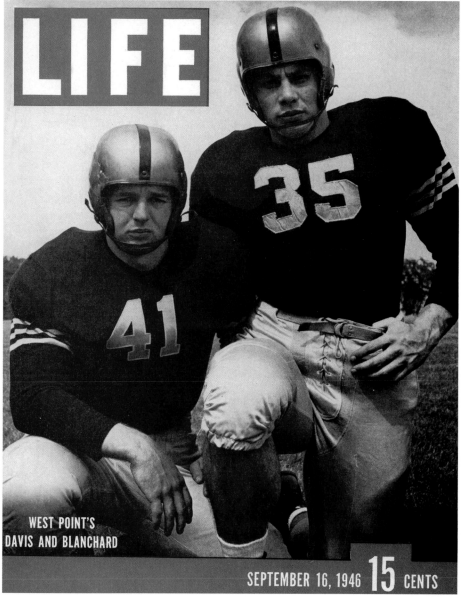

Their personalities were just as different. Nothing ever seemed to ruffle Blanchard. He was always a fun-loving, easygoing person who loved a good time and was a much more worldly country boy than the suburban-bred Davis. Glenn was dedicated and serious in his outlooks. He trained religiously, kept himself in perfect shape, never drank or smoked, and admitted that he was a "worrier." Though he always worked as hard as any cadet in his class to keep up, he worried about his studies. He worried about the games, even though his team was favored by at least two touchdowns in all but two games from 1944 through 1946—against Michigan and Notre Dame in 1946.

The only time Doc's teammates knew he was even a bit tense was when he talked in his sleep during the night before a game, yelling such things as, "There he goes! Tackle him! Get him!" Once while sleeping in a lower berth during a train trip to play a game, he began moving his legs as though he was churning through the line. The next morning, a teammate sleeping above him said he thought the train was coming apart.

When Blanchard and Davis came onto the nation's football stage in the fall of 1944, they were the perfect metaphor for the way in which America's armed forces were fighting and winning World War II. Their combination of power, speed, and agility mirrored the way their army brethren were spearheading an Allied force that was relentlessly rolling back the German army in western Europe and Italy with tactics much like those in a football playbook.

In the Pacific, army forces were supplementing the tenacity and firepower of the navy and marines in dismantling the expanded Japanese Empire, which had pushed itself more than halfway across the Pacific Ocean and had occupied huge areas on the mainland of Asia.

Many of these victorious U.S. forces were led by men who also had played football at West Point and who were using the lessons they learned from the sport—mobility, firepower, and shock action—to great advantage against their enemies. They had the perfect soul mates in Blanchard and Davis, and they exulted in every victory this pair helped to produce because the football victories were not unlike the successes they were achieving on the battlefield.

No commander was more visible than General of the Armies Dwight D. Eisenhower, the supreme allied commander in the European theater. He was a one-time Army back whose knee injury cut short his playing career and led him into coaching duties during his last two seasons at West Point. General Omar Bradley, one of his former teammates and a center on Army's unbeaten 1914 team, was in overall command of United States army ground forces in this mighty sweep. Both were members of the famed class of 1915, called "the Class of the Stars" because 58 of its 164 members became general officers. Many were former football players who did what football players seemed to do best during combat—they were in the midst of the fighting.

The 1914 team that was acclaimed national champions by the Helms Athletic Foundation was led by the Blanchard and Davis of its time, Vern Prichard, who later

AP/Wide World Photos

Dwight D. Eisenhower.

67

commanded the First and 14th Armored Divisions and who earned the Distinguished Service Medal and a Purple Heart, and Lou Merillat. They were Army's first outstanding passing combination.

The previous season, Army had been routed by Notre Dame when Knute Rockne and Gus Dorais stunned the Eastern football establishment with their uncanny use of the forward pass. Army coach Charley Daly adopted the strategy immediately for the Army-Navy game, and he had the perfect combination in Prichard and Merillat.

Early in the game, Merillat dropped a sure touchdown pass from Prichard. Merillat, an intense competitor, was so distraught at his mistake that he tried to bite the football and then threw himself on the ground and beat the turf with his fists.

Prichard laughed at this sight, and when Merillat returned to the huddle, he told him, "Forget it. There'll be plenty of other chances."

Doc Blanchard.

Downtown Athletic Club

There were. Prichard passed to Merillat for the go-ahead and clinching touchdowns, and running back Bill Hoge added the last score in a 22–9 victory.

From that 1914 football team of Eisenhower and Bradley also came a group of men who epitomized battlefield savvy and the special qualities of valor that underwrite the army's motto of "Duty, Honor, and Country."

Tom Larkin was a three-letterman who, as commander of the army's signal and special operations forces, won three Distinguished Service Medals, the Bronze Star, and Legion of Merit. Leland Hobbs, commander of the 30th Division from 1942 to 1945, won the Distinguished Service Medal, two Silver Stars, and three Bronze Stars. Roscoe Woodruff commanded the 77th Division, the 7th Corps, and the 24th Division in the Pacific theater of operations, during which he won two Distinguished Service Medals, three Silver Stars, two Bronze Stars, two Air Medals, and a Purple Heart.

There were others. Walter Hess, commander of the 36th Division artillery, won two Legion of Merit Medals and a pair of Bronze Stars. Hubert Harmon, commander of the 13th Air Force, won the Distinguished Service Medal and Distinguished Flying Cross and was the first superintendent of the Air Force Academy.

But no one surpassed James Van Fleet, a running back on that team. He won a Silver Star and Purple Heart in World War I; in World War II, he won 13 more major combat medals, including three Distinguished Service Crosses and two Purple Hearts as commander of the Eighth Infantry Regiment of the Fourth Division, assistant commander of the Second Division, and commanding general of both the Fourth and Ninetieth Divisions. During the Korean War, he commanded the Eighth Army in Korea for three years.

USMA Library Special Collections and Archives Division

The greatest running back tandem in college football history, Davis (left) and Blanchard.

Hoge earned a Distinguished Service Cross and a Silver Star as a young officer in World War I. During the early days of World War II, he was in charge of building the Alcan Highway, a vital road link between the continental United States and Alaska, over the rugged terrain of Canada. More than 60 years later, the road, in more modern form, is used by tens of thousands of tourists each year.

He was unsurpassed as a combat commander, attested to by his winning another Distinguished Service Cross and two more Silver Stars, plus two Distinguished Service Medals, the Legion of Merit, Bronze Star, Purple Heart, and Commendation Medal. He led both the Ninth and Fourth Armored Divisions in Africa, Sicily, and as part of General George S. Patton Jr.'s Third Army that roared across France and into Germany.

Patton was the battlefield version of Blaik. His tactics while commanding the Seventh Army in Africa and Sicily and the Third Army in western Europe might have been lifted from Blaik's playbook. He had gained a keen appreciation for the military applications of football during three years as a frustrated West Point player. Injuries had cost him the opportunity to win a varsity letter, and it rankled him forever.

However, it was not a total lost cause for him because he came away with greater respect for the correlation between football offense and battlefield tactics. He appreciated most of all the mind-set of the football-player-turned-commander that was always geared to attacking and defeating the enemy, just as they had attacked and tried to defeat opponents on the gridiron. That is why he had always sought former football players to lead his units and had great regard for leaders like Hoge; Prichard; Creighton Abrams, later the army's chief of staff; Bill Wood, who commanded the 13th Armored Division in the Rhineland and Central Europe; and Joe Gilbreath. All were former Army football players.

"Football attracts aggressive men, men who know what it takes to battle through a conflict to victory by utilizing the mobility and shock action that tank warfare also requires," he once wrote of the abilities former players brought to battle.

Blaik was also football's version of Patton. He underscored his football philosophy with the military tenet that his teams would always carry the attack. Thus, Army's running game, led by Blanchard and Davis, was not unlike Patton's ground forces attacking the enemy through swift, sledgehammer attacks led by his armored units tearing open an enemy's battle line. That was Blanchard ripping through the line of scrimmage and scattering defenders as he tore into the secondary en route to big gains or touchdowns. The blinding speed of Davis' end runs easily translated into the way Patton's forces swept enemy flanks with tanks and infantry en route to huge advances.

Patton supplemented these ground maneuvers with an insistence that his forces be given solid air cover, which in Army's football philosophy was Tucker's passing game backing off opposing secondaries from trying to stop Blanchard and Davis.

Red Blaik (holding the football) was football's version of General Patton.

That just underscored the mantra put forth long before World War II by the one-time manager of the 1902 Army football team, General Douglas MacArthur, and still carved upon the wall of West Point's old gymnasium: "Upon the fields of friendly strife, are sown the seeds that, upon other fields, in other days, will bear the fruits of victory."

MacArthur further amplified it when, upon being presented with the National Football Foundation and Hall of Fame's Gold Medal in 1959, he said:

"Football has become a symbol of courage, stamina, and coordinated efficiency. In war and peace, I have found football men to be my greatest reliance."

Like Patton, he had learned firsthand from watching the careers of players who were members of his 1902 team, particularly men who became skilled coaches like Bunker, Ernest "Pot" Graves, and Charley Daly. They later coached Merillat, Prichard, Hoge, and some of the other future combat leaders and then became their mentors. Graves, who also was a pioneer in line play, later became known as the "Father of the Engineers." Around the Pentagon during World War II, he was referred to as "the colonel who wears civilian clothes." The civilian garb was a concession to his ability to simplify engineering problems that baffled others.

Ralph Sasse was another person who could simplify engineering problems that baffled others. He had played football with Bradley and Van Fleet before graduating from West Point in 1916, and a year later, he was the first American combat officer to step on French soil in World War I. He commanded the 301st Tank Battalion

Blanchard helps Davis adjust his pads while dressing for a game.

"Mr. Outside" running outside.

and was cited by the British for his heroism. He later joined Patton and Eisenhower as part of a group who urged the army to establish a separate armored corps. Their ideas were shot down by the army's infantry and horse cavalry traditionalists, but the men later proved themselves prophets as American armored forces swept across western Europe to help win World War II.

Sasse played a large role in the development of the army's armored units, and he later was called from a brief retirement to help train those units. One of his great disappointments was not being able to join them in combat. There was a unanimity of opinion among those who knew his talent for leading armored forces, built around the same philosophy he used in leading his football teams, that he would have rivaled Patton in the success of American tank warfare during World War II.

Patton never disagreed. In fact, he said very bluntly, "I would rather have Sasse serving under me or I serve him, than any other officer in the army."

Sasse had been just as dynamic a coach at Army from 1930 to 1931 as he was a player. His style obviously rubbed off on his three team captains, who distinguished themselves during World War II. The 1930 team captain, Charles Humber, commanded the 31st Infantry Battalion in the battle of Bataan until its ammunition and supplies were nearly exhausted and it was forced to surrender to the overwhelming Japanese forces. He survived the Bataan Death March and continued to provide critical leadership for his men until he died aboard a POW ship in 1945.

John Price, captain of the 1931 team and a two-time All-American tackle, commanded the Army Air Force's 460th Heavy Bombardment Group and won a Distinguished Flying Cross and two Air Medals; in the Korean War, he was deputy commander of the air force's 35th Air Division and was awarded the Distinguished Service Medal and the Navy Cross.

Milt Summerfelt, an All-American guard and captain of the 1932 team, commanded the 333rd Heavy Bombardment Group on Okinawa and won the Legion of Merit and Commendation Ribbon.

The Heisman Seasons

Patton's successful style of warfare was easily recognizable on the gridiron in 1944–1946 in the Blanchard and Davis teams. It also carried Blaik's distinctive coaching trademark, one that made him Army's most successful football coach ever. Throughout his career, first at Dartmouth and then for 18 seasons at West Point, his teams were meticulously drilled. A West Point graduate himself, he firmly believed that playing for West Point was a singular honor.

"He was high class all the way, and so were the men who worked for him as assistant coaches," Davis said. "They were wonderful men, great teachers and totally talented in what they did. That's why so many of them became great head coaches after they left his staff.

Coach Blaik with Blanchard and Davis.

USMA Library Special Collections and Archives Division

"He didn't permit any swearing, by coaches or players, on the practice field, nor did he like a coach bawling out a player in front of his teammates. If there were criticisms to be made, the coach took the player to the sideline, away from everyone, and straightened him out. Those men were great examples to all of us of what intelligent leadership was about."

"The colonel [as all of his players referred to him] kept our feet on the ground," said Blanchard, "because he didn't have much use for all the notoriety on our team. Maybe any other team would have gotten carried away, but he didn't allow that to happen. Part of the reason was that we accepted pretty much everything he told us, and we had tremendous respect for him and for his strong value system. We still revere his memory, and all of us still seem to quote him about once a day."

Blaik was a soft-spoken man, who rarely raised his voice on the practice field. He was blunt, a straight talker who was easy to understand. Before a game, as his players lay resting on mats in their locker room, he'd walk in and say, "Are you ready?"

"Oh, we were ready," Blanchard said. "He had seen to that during the week because our practices were not only meticulously run but often very intense. He was never satisfied unless we had done everything to his satisfaction. We didn't have a lot of plays, but everything we had was geared to make us successful. He believed that repetition was one of the keys to performance, and what he did best was to have his players take what he had taught them and then make it work."

When Blaik unveiled his 1944 football team, it was a mirror image of its combat brethren. Actually, there were two teams so deep, talented, and powerful that it was hard to distinguish one from the other. Blanchard and Davis were assigned to the second unit, comprised mostly of plebes, except for quarterback and team captain Tom Lombardo.

The first backfield included quarterback Doug Kenna, plus running backs Max Minor, Dale Hall, and Glenn Dobbs, all returning lettermen. This unit was among the best in the nation, and though it started every game that season, it soon played second fiddle in the public's mind to the Blanchard and Davis group. Blaik gave each team equal playing time, with the plebe unit playing mostly in the second and fourth quarters. If Army had to kick off to start a game, then Blanchard did the job and played for a time with Kenna's unit. He left before the end of the first quarter then returned in the second quarter with Lombardo's team because the rules forbade a player leaving the game and returning in the same quarter.

"I had the distinct privilege of watching the two best teams, and some of the best college players in the country, every week when they scrimmaged each other," Blaik once said. "It was often tempting to let them go longer than we planned because they were so special."

Ed Rafalko was a senior tackle on Kenna's team, but he got a good taste of what it was like to play against Blanchard during midweek scrimmages. "We played both ways, and when we scrimmaged Doc's team, he made no distinctions as to whether it was a practice or a game," said Rafalko. He played with our unit for a time if he had to kick off. You'd better make your block and get out of the way because when he came through, he didn't make any distinction for friend or foe. If you were in his way, he'd run over you, and that was on offense as well as defense. He was one of the toughest players we had."

Rafalko recalled the 1944 season's fifth game against Duke when Army trailed 7–6 at halftime, the only time all year that it was behind. "We weren't playing as well as we should, and at halftime Colonel Blaik told us that we were going to run the ball, but only between the ends, no sweeps or fancy-Dan stuff," he said. "That was Blanchard's style of game, and when he got into the game, it was something to watch him work because he was a player who seemed to love contact. He was never happier than when he was taking it to someone.

"We won the game 27–7, and it was the turning point of the season because no one could handle us from then on."

Lombardo, a splendid team leader, played a big role in that achievement. Normally, a team captain who is quarterback would lead the most experienced unit. But Blaik wanted his leadership and stability to guide the plebe unit because most of them were just getting used to playing with each other. Unlike other college freshman teams, this one was older, and many of its members already had played college football. Lombardo obviously did a splendid job because his Blanchard and Davis unit helped Army outscore its opponents 504–35 for a 9–0 record and the national championship.

Lombardo also was a regimental officer, and one of his jobs was inspecting Davis' room every day. Glenn didn't take very seriously much of West Point's caste system for cadets of different classes, and he often drove Lombardo wild by kidding around while Tom was very seriously going about his business. Occasionally, Davis became too casual and Lombardo made him do push-ups. One time, Davis teased him so badly that the push-up count reportedly got to 120. Davis, always in superb physical condition, didn't flinch and ripped them off as if there was nothing to it.

Sadly, Lombardo paid the ultimate price during the early months of the Korean War. Five days after assuming command of I Company of the Second Division's Thirty-eighth Infantry Regiment, which had helped American forces break out of the Pusan Perimeter, he was killed leading his company in a battle to seize a hilltop near Chogye, Korea, the first, but certainly not the last, Army football player to die in that war. Lombardo Field has always been the site of American football games at Yongsan Reservation in Seoul, Korea. In a message sent to the dedication service in 1962, Blaik noted: "From her sons, West Point expects the best—Tom Lombardo always gave his best."

The 1944 team was special, made more so by the emergence of Blanchard and Davis as an overwhelming force. Playing sometimes little more than a quarter, and rarely more than a half, Blanchard had nine touchdowns and made more than seven yards each time he carried the ball. One of his most spectacular plays came against his former school, North Carolina. Davis threw a three-yard option pass to end Barney Poole. He was immediately surrounded by potential tacklers, so he lateraled the ball to Blanchard, and Doc sprinted 60 yards untouched for the touchdown in a 46–0 victory.

Davis was a stunning performer, easily the most exciting college player in the nation that year. He scored three touchdowns each against major opponents North Carolina, Brown, Notre Dame, Villanova, and Pennsylvania. At season's end, he was the country's leading scorer with 120 points from 20 touchdowns—records that still stand at West Point.

Quarterback and team captain Tom Lombardo.

USMA Library Special Collections and Archives Division

In their two greatest victories that year, over Notre Dame and Navy, Blanchard and Davis were immense. On the same day that Patton's Third Army rolled up a tremendous victory by surrounding the fortress city of Metz, the Army football team crushed Notre Dame, 59–0. That was more points than Army had scored against the Irish in the previous 15 seasons combined, and the first since 1938. The third-ranked Irish were well stocked with players from other colleges who were members of the Navy's V-12 officer training program, but this didn't stop Irish scout Jack Lavelle, who had watched Army demolish Villanova 83–0 the previous week, from giving this succinct report for coach Ed McKeever: "Cancel the game!"

A Yankee Stadium crowd of 75,000 (Army said it could have sold 200,000 tickets) was awestruck as the Cadets, though outweighed by the Irish, led 20–0 after 11 minutes. Davis' interception set up a fourth touchdown early in the second quarter en route to a 33–0 halftime lead. Davis scored three touchdowns, and it hardly mattered that Blanchard didn't score at all because his blocking and defense spoke just as loudly.

"The game got out of hand because Notre Dame did a lot of stupid, frantic things trying to keep up with us," said Blanchard, who had one of eight Army interceptions that set up three touchdowns.

"The scores were never indicative of just how good those Notre Dame teams were in 1944 and 1945," Davis said. "They had some fine players, many who later played on their 1946 team that shared the national championship with us. We got 'em on the run both years and kept it that way. We certainly didn't dominate the statistics because we made a lot of long plays."

Former Army player Gus Farwick, fighting in the Appenine Mountains in Italy, heard the score over shortwave radio. "Just a lot of damned German propaganda," he declared. A month later, "59–0" became one of the countersigns that army forces used for identification to prevent German forces, dressed in American uniforms, from infiltrating their lines during the Battle of the Bulge.

If Army needed any additional emotional support to beat Notre Dame, it came from dedicating the game to Colonel Russell P. Reeder Jr. A former Army end in the twenties, he was flown to New York from Washington's Walter Reed Army Hospital in the private plane of army Chief of Staff General George C. Marshall. Reeder sat in a wheelchair, with the lower part of his body wrapped in a white blanket that didn't allow the crowd to see that he had lost part of his left leg at Normandy shortly after D-Day while commanding the Fourth Division's Eleventh Regiment. Later, he became the "soul" of West Point athletics, an inspiration to thousands of Cadets with whom he came in contact during his two decades as assistant director of athletics.

Three weeks later, and after a 62–7 thrashing of eighth-ranked Penn, the Cadets played Navy for the national championship. The game originally had been scheduled to be played at the Naval Academy, as it had been in 1942, as a symbolic gesture to promote rationing of gasoline, tires, and automobiles and cutting down on civilian use of much-needed rail space for the movement of troops and supplies.

79

Blanchard signs autographs at the Heisman Award ceremony.

80

Downtown Athletic Club

But the Sixth War Bond Drive, to finance the last campaigns of the war, was about to begin, and President Franklin D. Roosevelt was sold on the idea of moving the game to Baltimore's 65,000-seat Municipal Stadium. It was Navy's home away from home, and admission to all those seats was by war bond purchase only. Everything was arranged within just three weeks, and the game raised nearly $60 million, the most for any war bond event during World War II.

Navy even helped Army's Corps of Cadets to get to the game, supplying a troop ship that sailed from the south dock at West Point, down the Hudson River, and into the still–German U-boat infested Atlantic Ocean off the East Coast. Navy warships guarded the ship, and submarine hunting planes and blimps looked down from the skies until it reached the mouth of the Chesapeake Bay and sailed north to Baltimore. The procedure was repeated right after the game. However, it was no "fun cruise," despite Army's 23–7 victory that achieved a national championship. A furious storm battered the ship when it was halfway down Chesapeake Bay until it turned into New York Harbor and headed back up the Hudson River. The victorious football team, though, rode home smoothly on the train.

The ride wasn't as smooth as the Cadets' victory. "We played a team that was equal to us physically, and that's what it was—a very physical game," Blanchard said. "We didn't change anything we did nor was there a lot of hoopla because we knew this was a big game by itself. Despite our great successes, our team was very self-

Downtown Athletic Club

Glenn Davis is honored at the Heisman Award ceremony as his coach, Red Blaik (center), and the president of the Downtown Athletic Club look on.

81

motivated, and when Navy began talking about what their great line was going to do to us, our linemen got so hopped up, we could barely contain them."

The game belonged to Blanchard and Davis who, for a change, weren't given a seat because of a runaway. Army led just 9–7 going into the last quarter before Davis' interception keyed a 52-yard scoring drive. In seven carries, Blanchard gained all but four yards, roaring through an enormous hole opened by guard Art Gerometta and center Herschel "Ug" Fuson for the last 10 yards for a touchdown that put Army ahead 16–7.

The next time Army got the ball, it went 69 yards for another score. The last 50 yards were by Davis on a sweep to the right called "the California Special," put in the game plan especially for him. Crushing blocks by end Barney Poole and running back Max Minor cleared his way. He left a frustrated trail of would-be tacklers in his wake as he scored his 20th touchdown and capped Army's first victory over Navy in five years.

Half a world away, in the Philippines, Lieutenant General Robert L. Eichelberger, who had hired Blaik to resuscitate West Point's sagging football program three years earlier and who was then commanding the U.S. Army's invasion of Leyte Island, listened to the game on his radio during the wee hours of Sunday morning, local time. Afterward, he and some of his staff slogged through the muddy terrain in a jeep and up to the front lines to tell the good news to Colonel Charles

"Monk" Meyer, one of Army's great running backs during the thirties. He was leading the Second Battalion, 127th Infantry Regiment of the 32nd Division in fierce fighting against Japanese forces. Even the war took a temporary backseat as they briefly celebrated the momentous victory and the national championship.

A few hours later in Baltimore, Blaik was handed a telegram. It read: "The greatest of all Army teams. We have stopped the war to celebrate your magnificent success. MacArthur."

Davis won the prestigious Maxwell Trophy as Player of the Year and gained a similar award from the Helms Athletic Foundation. Both Blanchard and Davis were unanimous All-America selections, and they finished second and third in the Heisman Trophy voting behind Les Horvath of the unbeaten Ohio State Buckeyes.

Davis later wrote: "Of the many thrills I've had, I suppose the Army-Navy game of 1944 gave me my greatest. We at West Point considered that victory the best of our winning streak."

The 1945 season began two weeks after World War II ended with MacArthur, the 1902 Army football manager, presiding at the unconditional surrender of Japan aboard the USS *Missouri* in Tokyo Bay. That season, with just one unit instead of two, Blanchard and Davis were the driving forces for what Blaik and many believed was the greatest team in college football history to that time, and it certainly was unmatched in the history of the Military Academy—then and now. The team proved its greatness by winning a second straight national championship with another perfect season.

Though Blanchard and Davis scored 37 of the team's 61 touchdowns, this was Doc's year. He averaged seven yards for each of his 101 rushing attempts; his four pass receptions gained 166 yards, an amazing 41.5 yards per catch; he had four interceptions, three for touchdowns; and he led the team in touchdowns with 19, one more than Davis. Away from football, in the previous April, he was chosen as a member of a special cadet honor guard at the funeral of President Franklin D. Roosevelt.

The first test for Blanchard and Davis was in the season's third game against a young but very talented Michigan team at Yankee Stadium. Some 70,000 watched a great performance by Blanchard and Davis against Michigan's separate offensive and defensive units—the start of two-platoon football. For the first time, Blanchard and Davis faced a defense that did not have tired and battered two-way players. But that didn't seem to matter because they cut Michigan to pieces in a 28–7 victory.

A week after Army had beaten Duke, 27–7, famed CBS radio sportscaster Ted Husing arrived at the Blue Devils' campus to broadcast a game, and he was rushed over to meet one of the Duke players. "You have to meet this fellow," he was breathlessly told. "He stopped Doc Blanchard." The lad, Kelly Mote, had tackled Blanchard behind the line of scrimmage for a one-yard loss, and despite his team's loss, that play had made him a campus hero.

Blanchard and Davis led a 48–0 humiliation of an unbeaten Notre Dame team a few weeks later before another sellout crowd of 75,000 at Yankee Stadium. Few

Charles "Monk" Meyer.

"Monk" Meyer

outside the Notre Dame campus knew that Frank Leahy, who had coached the team to a national championship in 1943 and who was supposed to be on full-time active duty with the navy at the huge Fleet City base near San Francisco, was coaching the team each week. Hugh Devore was the nominal coach, but Leahy flew to Notre Dame and coached the team from Monday until Thursday. He then returned to Fleet City, leaving Devore to handle the game-day work.

His handiwork was clearly evident in the way that Notre Dame played before it met Army. But there was nothing Leahy could have done to prepare it for Blanchard and Davis. Davis scored on a 26-yard run on Army's third play; he got number two on a 31-yard pass from Tucker and number three on an amazing 21-yard run in which he reversed his field and then weaved untouched through would-be tacklers.

Blanchard scored twice, his second touchdown coming on a 36-yard interception return. That gave Army a 35–0 lead before the midway point of the third quarter. Once again, with such an overwhelming lead, Blaik pulled his two stars, and, in a very rare show of disgust, Davis threw away his helmet.

"Heck, Colonel," he said to Blaik, "I want to play football and you're not giving me a chance."

Blaik did not anticipate such a rout by his team against an unbeaten Notre Dame team. But, as happened against every overmatched opponent when Army got big leads, he did not want to be accused of running up scores. He didn't remonstrate against Davis for his mild case of insubordination. In fact, it pleased him to see that his star players were still so motivated despite having the game won long before it was over.

The question has always been raised of just how great Blanchard and Davis' statistics and records might have been had they recorded more playing time. They played less than half of the 1944 season and just over half of the 1945 season. Certainly, rolling up statistics in games that ceased to be competitive would have tainted any records, but what they achieved was against the best possible competition on a schedule that had been largely set for several years. It was by no means a walkover because in 1944, Army played four teams ranked no lower than 11th; and in 1945, six of their nine opponents were ranked in the top 20, including four in the top 10.

As if to confront the question directly, after routing Notre Dame, Blanchard and Davis scored five touchdowns the following week in a 61–0 rout of once-beaten and nationally ranked Penn. Once again, they spent most of the second half watching from the bench. That game, Blaik always maintained, was the apex of their greatness.

In the first period, Blanchard actually scored three times in one series, but the first two were wiped away by penalty. It didn't matter because on the second and third attempts, he made up the extra distance tacked on by each penalty on each extra try, and when his third one finally counted, he shouted to Davis, "Thank God, they counted this score."

At the Army-Navy game, which again decided the national championship, President Harry S Truman was the first chief executive since Calvin Coolidge, in 1925, to attend the classic. It also was televised for the first time to a select few who had television sets in New York City, Philadelphia, and Schenectady, New York.

Blanchard was at his greatest against the undefeated and second-ranked Mids. He scored Army's first two touchdowns, the second on a 17-yard run in which he went through Navy's Clyde Scott, in Blaik's words, "as if he were an animated rain cloud." With Blanchard leading the way with his blocking, Davis ran 49 yards for a touchdown, and the Cadets led 20–0 at the end of the first quarter. In the second half, Blanchard notched his third interception return for a touchdown—the first player in the modern era to score three touchdowns in Army-Navy competition—and Davis capped the momentous 32–13 victory with a 28-yard touchdown run.

Blanchard's cousin, Ed Tatum, came to the locker room after the game to congratulate him for his great performance. But Doc didn't want to talk about the game.

"He was there, Ed," Blanchard said. "I could feel him patting me on the back after each play and saying, 'Hit like your old daddy did, son.'"

Blanchard was referring to his father, "Big Doc," who had died before he ever saw his son play for Army. Nonetheless, Doc always carried his dad's memory with him on the field. He played as much to win for Army as he did to please his father, who had been so instrumental in getting him to West Point and who, more than anyone else, would have appreciated the manner in which he played the game.

85

A few days after the Army-Navy game, Blanchard received a telegram from the Downtown Athletic Club (DAC) in New York City, informing him that he had won the Heisman Trophy, the first player from either service academy to be so honored.

"That was it," he remembered. "There were no TVs in our rooms at that time, and we didn't have much time to listen to the radio or read the newspapers, so I really wasn't aware of the Heisman Trophy. And there certainly wasn't the hype associated with the trophy as there is today."

He went to New York City to receive the award from the DAC's Wilfred Wottrich in a very modest ceremony, accompanied by Blaik and West Point's sports information director, Joe Cahill. He sent it home to his mother in Bishopville, South Carolina, and there it stayed for most of his quarter century in the Air Force as Doc and his family moved from base to base. Today, it sits in the home of his daughter in Bulverde, Texas, where Doc, now a widower, resides.

"People who came to our house liked to touch it and rub it," he said. "It is special to them, and it still is very special to me."

In 1945, he also was a unanimous All-American for the second straight year and won the Maxwell Award and the Walter Camp Trophy as the Player of the Year. He became the first college football player ever given the Sullivan Award, presented annually to the nation's best amateur athlete.

Blanchard had to be truly great to win the 1945 Heisman because Davis, who finished second in the voting for the second time in a row, had the best season of his career, tying his 11.5-yards-per-carry record, which still stands, from the previous year. He also had his best rushing season with 944 yards and set a total offense record of 11.7 yards per play.

When the 1946 season began, the halcyon days of absolute dominance that had marked 1944 and 1945 were replaced by a huge question mark of just how Blanchard and Davis would fare in a college football landscape that had drastically changed with colleges back on a full peacetime footing. Football talent at civilian schools overflowed from the sudden release of five years' worth of potential players whose gridiron careers had been deterred by wartime service. Conversely, there was a drastic change at West Point, where only nine starters from 1945 returned to play in 1946. Its talent pool had dropped considerably from its 1944 and 1945 levels because many of the stars from those teams either graduated or resigned their appointments to return to civilian schools.

"We had our weakest of the three great teams," Davis said. "We certainly didn't enjoy the riches of 1944 and 1945. That team was special in its own way, and it was a real tribute to its players that we won, even if it wasn't in the overwhelming manner of the previous two years."

Worse still, the heart of Army's offensive line—Coulter, John Green, and Al Nemetz, plus Ug Fuson who was moved from center to fullback, for a time—were gone. There were no easy pickings on Army's schedule. The Cadets played four nationally ranked teams, including co-national champion Notre Dame. All of this was made even harder by the "payback time" mood directed at Blanchard and Davis. All the pundits predicted that they would find it much tougher to dominate the game than they had the two previous seasons.

But they delivered their answer to all the naysayers with a third straight unbeaten season—marred only by a scoreless tie against mighty Notre Dame—and a national championship ranking in several polls. In a few other polls, Notre Dame was acclaimed the champion. Only a surprisingly close 21–18 victory over a woeful Navy team in the final game of their career cost them a third straight undisputed title.

"It was by no means easy," Blanchard remembers. "We had only the remnants of the 1944 team, and what made matters worse, our gritty little band had 16 players who played hurt the entire season. I had a shoulder separation and knee injury that today would be diagnosed as a partially torn anterior cruciate ligament. But I missed just two games."

The knee injury occurred in the season's opening game against Villanova at West Point. Blanchard was twisting away from a tackler, and, while trying to regain top speed, he was hit on the shoulders by a defender. His foot sunk in a soggy playing surface, and his knee, instead of bending inward as he fell, bent in the opposite direction. Two sets of ligaments were torn, and one of them pulled off a small piece of bone. It was an injury serious enough to keep most players out of action for an entire season.

But Blanchard's fantastic calf and thigh development acted as a shock absorber and deflected the serious damage. It caused him to miss hard-fought victories over

Oklahoma and Cornell, and while he returned after those games to play the entire rest of the season, he was never the same overwhelming player of the two previous years. He no longer kicked off or punted, and he was held out of weekly scrimmages to protect the knee. His carries increased by 20 percent, but his rushing average slipped a couple of yards. Still, that didn't prevent him from being named unanimously to the All-America team for the third straight season.

Blaik later wrote of the effect of Blanchard's injury:

"His determination and an unusual quadriceps-muscle group enabled him, with a minimum amount of exercise, to stabilize the knee sufficiently to play. But all year long, we were harassed by the fear that the knee might go at any time. Doc was never his '44 or '45 self by 40 percent . . . but even at 60 percent efficiency, he was a heckuva player."

Blanchard's hopes of winning back-to-back Heisman Trophies were dashed.

"Heck, if I hadn't gotten hurt in 1946, I might have been the first Archie Griffin," Blanchard said, chuckling at the prospect of becoming the first two-time Heisman Trophy winner as Griffin did in the seventies.

Davis assumed more of the offensive and defensive workload in 1946, and he had an incredible season. In addition to carrying the rushing load for two games while Blanchard was sidelined, by the fifth game, he was the team's punter and became its long passer after Tucker separated his right shoulder and sprained his right elbow and wrist on the fourth play of the game against Michigan. For the rest of the season, Tucker's injury didn't allow him to raise his arm far enough above his shoulder to do any long passing. That role fell to Davis through a series of option passes. He got the ball either on a direct snap through Tucker's legs while he stood behind the quarterback, or Tucker took the ball, whirled, and tossed Davis a backward pass. He then had the option to run or pass. He completed 19 of 47 for a career-best 396 yards and four touchdowns. On defense, Davis picked up as much slack as possible without jeopardizing the overall play of the secondary because Tucker's injuries limited his superb defensive skills.

Blanchard returned to play against Michigan, a game many of the nation's sports pundits predicted would spell the end of the Blanchard-Davis dominance. Davis was never better. He ran a trap play 59 yards for a tie-making touchdown late in the first quarter, zigzagging his way past a bevy of would-be tacklers without being touched.

With time about to expire in the first half, he struck again with the play of the day—maybe of the year—shortly after Blanchard's leaping 44-yard catch of his pass that put Army into Michigan territory. On fourth down, as Tucker whirled to toss the ball back to Davis for a halfback option pass to reserve end Bob Folsom, he was hit by Michigan's players, and the ball came loose and bounced along the ground. Instinctively, Davis seized it, pushed away a couple of Michigan linemen, and threw a pass to Folsom, who made a leaping catch in the end zone. Army led, 13–7.

In the fourth quarter, with the scored tied 13–13, Blanchard and Davis made it look like old times during a game-winning 76-yard drive. They hooked up on a

87

key pass, and Blanchard then took Army to a 20–13 victory, stomping the final seven yards around left end for the winning touchdown while he carried a Michigan defensive player on his back for the final three yards.

"It was my first game back after being injured, and I know that Colonel Blaik took a chance in his mind by starting me because he wasn't sure just how well my knee would hold up," Blanchard said. "It worked out because we hung on and did the best we could until we could finally beat them in the fourth quarter. The game's key play was Glenn's touchdown pass to Bob Folsom at the end of the first half. It was tough against such a superbly coached team, but we proved to everyone, including ourselves, that we still were good enough to beat the nation's best team, even though it took some luck."

Davis may have won the Heisman Trophy that day with his great all-around performance, one that Blaik later called "his best game ever at West Point," and that was saying something considering his many great games. He ran for 105 yards, completed seven of eight passes for 168 yards, ran 59 yards for one touchdown, passed for the second, and was a key player in the game-winning drive with his running and passing. There no longer was any doubt that Davis and Blanchard, even with the latter playing on one good leg, were just as spectacular against great postwar teams.

A few weeks later, after a four-touchdown game by Blanchard against Columbia, including a 92-yard kickoff return that was like the Doc of old, the entire nation was riveted to the "game of the century" when Army played Notre Dame in Yankee Stadium. Army athletic director, Colonel Lawrence "Biff" Jones, said that if Yankee Stadium had a million seats instead of 75,000, he could have filled all of them. As it was, Notre Dame had to refund a half million dollars' worth of unfilled ticket orders.

They were the country's two best teams. Army was a slight underdog to what was to that point the most powerful Notre Dame team ever. Most of the pundits and so-called experts said that Blanchard and Davis would at last find an opponent too strong for them to defeat. Added to that edge was the "revenge factor" that was driving Notre Dame and many of its players who had played in the humiliating losses in 1944 and 1945.

No one at the time could recall a game like it. West Point's athletic department was flooded with messages promising revenge of the highest magnitude, such as the letter that read:

"Army, beware! Only 40 days left until Notre Dame gets sweet revenge. Oh, what a beating your Cadets are going to take. Good-bye winning streak."

It was signed, "The Fighting Irish."

Unfortunately, the pregame hype was more exciting than the game because nothing was settled as the teams played to a scoreless tie. Both Blaik and Notre Dame coach Frank Leahy admitted afterward that they played not to lose rather than allowing their great players to perform at their best. The Irish defense was so intent on holding Davis in check that it keyed three or four defenders on his every move. Of course, 11 turnovers by both teams precluded either team from maintaining serious scoring drives.

"That was a game nobody seemed to want to win or lose," Blanchard recalled. "I broke a good play late in the third quarter and thought I could score, but Johnny Lujack got me after a 21-yard gain into Notre Dame territory."

From his own 42-yard line, Blanchard had run a counterplay to the right, and all the Army defenders followed the other two backs, Davis and Rip Rowan, as they headed to the left. Blanchard quickly broke through the line, and the only defender barring him from the end zone was Lujack, the Irish safety. Lujack hit him head-on, and as his arms started to slip down and Blanchard started to pull away, he frantically grabbed one of Doc's feet and tripped him at the Irish 36-yard line.

That was Army's best shot. If there was an edge by either team, it belonged to the Cadets who were inside Notre Dame's 30-yard line six times, compared to just three trips over midfield by Notre Dame for the entire game. The Irish had the game's best scoring shot, reaching Army's 4-yard line in the second quarter before the Cadets stopped a fourth-down end run.

According to legend and lore from that game, in the game's final minute, the story goes, Blanchard leaped and caught a pass from Davis as he was covered by Pete Ashbaugh, a former B-29 pilot during World War II.

"Get it, Doc! Get it!" Davis yelled at Blanchard. After Blanchard caught the ball, Ashbaugh said to him, "Nice catch, Doc. Too bad you're out of bounds." Blanchard looked down and saw that his legs were indeed straddling the sideline and just laughed.

A week later, Army blasted Penn 34–7. Blanchard scored one touchdown; Davis passed for one and scored two others. Early in the game, Davis' head hit the ground after a tackle, but he continued to play without incident. After scoring his second touchdown, he asked Tucker why the play on which he had just scored hadn't been used in the game. At first, the Army quarterback thought he was joking, but he soon discovered that Glenn had forgotten scoring the touchdown and much of the action that had preceded it. He had performed brilliantly on sheer instinct and short-term memory.

Of course, Tucker told Blaik, and the coach immediately took Davis out of the game. Davis, still not comprehending his plight, immediately protested.

"What are you taking me out for, Colonel?" he asked. "What did I do wrong?" Blaik tried to assure him that he hadn't made any mistakes. But it wasn't until later in the third quarter, when he had regained his senses, that he returned to the game and scored another touchdown. He almost had a fourth score when, during a punt return, he ran 35 yards before being surrounded by would-be tacklers. He then lateraled the ball to tackle Harold Tavzel, who ran 44 yards for the touchdown.

Army played its traditional game against Navy two weeks later and was a prohibitive three-touchdown favorite because Navy had won just one game that season. Naturally, everyone expected that the Blanchard-Davis era would conclude with the two players riding out in a blaze of glory. What no one ever expected was that the game would rank with the greatest the two teams ever played against each other—indeed, it would become one of the greatest games in college football history.

"Everything looked easy when we scored three touchdowns in the first half," Blanchard said. "In the second half, we seemed to be waiting for things to happen rather than taking the fight to them. Once that started, we never got it going again."

A sellout crowd of 102,000 jammed Philadelphia's Municipal Stadium, most of them to render a final salute to Blanchard and Davis. Glenn didn't disappoint them as he caught a 13-yard touchdown pass from Tucker on Army's first possession. Though the huge crowd, including President Truman and his family, didn't realize it at the time, the underdog Mids flashed a preview of what would come by then scoring on their first possession. They missed the extra point—something that eventually cost them the game.

On Army's next series, Blanchard tore off a 52-yard touchdown run, and Davis then used his favorite halfback option pass to connect on a 26-yard scoring pass to Doc for a 21–6 halftime lead. No one realized it at the time, because it seemed as if Army would add more touchdowns, but that was the final time the Blanchard-Davis combination would score for Army. In retrospect, it was only fitting that their final touchdown—the 89th in their three seasons together—should be a shared experience.

But in the Army dressing room, the talk centered on how many points could still be scored. "You could hear such remarks as, 'Let's make it 50–6' and 'they couldn't break a paper bag the way they're blocking today,'" Davis remembered. "We all seemed to be wondering how the newspapers would play up a 50–6 game and didn't take the second half seriously because they rammed it right down our throats."

Navy owned the second half, and it took Blanchard and Davis right out of the game. The Mids scored midway through the third quarter and again missed the extra point, to trail 21–12. The game's biggest play occurred early in the fourth quarter. On fourth and inches at Army's 34-yard line, Blaik disdained a punt, and Blanchard was stopped in his tracks on fourth down. Navy immediately seized the momentum and scored again but missed its third extra point and trailed 21–18.

The game reached its frantic conclusion when a last-ditch Navy drive put the ball at Army's 3-yard line with 90 seconds to play. But the Cadets were desperate, not only to preserve a victory but also to maintain the unbeaten record of this great era. Davis has never forgotten the moment. "I got our guys in a huddle and said, 'Listen, everything we did for the last three years will be lost if we let these guys beat us.'"

Two Navy runs were stopped cold, and the Mids, with no timeouts remaining, called one illegally to try and organize a scoring play. They were penalized five yards back to the 8-yard line.

By this time, thousands from the huge crowd had surged onto the sidelines and spilled over onto the playing field. Guards frantically moved them back inside the sideline marker when Navy's Bill Hawkins, who had led the Mids' gallant drive, faked a line plunge, then shoveled the ball out to halfback Pete Williams. He tried to turn end Barney Poole's corner. Helped by Blanchard at linebacker, they forced Williams to run ever wider toward the sideline. Soon, Poole and Williams disappeared into the sea of fans that had again obliterated the sideline stripe. Officials dove into the pile and immediately ruled that Williams had not gone out of bounds when he was tackled at the 5-yard line. Before Navy could get organized for a last fourth-down play, the clock ran off its final seconds, and Army won the game, 21–18.

The Blanchard-Davis era had ended on a successful, albeit very scary, note. Not that it would have changed the outcome, but the question of whether the crowd prevented the officials from correctly deciding whether Williams went out of bounds—and did or did not stop the clock that would have given Navy one last play—has always hovered over the game's ending, except at West Point, because game films did not give a decisive view of the play's ending.

It was left for Army's Joe Steffy, who played nearly 60 minutes in the game, to place things in context: "Army won the game, and Navy thought it did," he said.

There was a bit of irony in that frantic finish. Blanchard and Davis, the greatest offensive backfield tandem of all time, finished their career by using all of their energies on defense in the final minutes of their last game together to help their team salvage a victory. When it was achieved, they walked off the field as nearly invisible participants in one of the great games for the ages, their achievements only momentarily overshadowed by Navy's heroic effort to create one of the biggest upsets in college football history.

By season's end, the pundits and public alike fully appreciated Davis' great all-around talent, and he won the Heisman Trophy; Blanchard finished fourth in the voting. Davis' durability was without question because he averaged 57 minutes a game during the season, playing every minute of games against Michigan, Notre Dame, and Navy when the team's unbeaten streak was on the line. He was on the field for 55 minutes against Oklahoma and Duke. His total offense against much stronger competition was just 89 yards shy of what he had achieved in 1945.

When Davis graduated the following June, he was awarded the Hughes Trophy as the football team's most valuable player in 1946. "I've always said that I'm more proud of graduating from West Point than anything else I've ever done," he said later.

When Glenn was an executive at the *Los Angeles Times*, two of his suburban neighbors were Heisman winners Tom Harmon (1940) and Les Horvath (1944). Each of them had their trophies displayed in the living areas of their homes. A new neighbor who attended several social functions at their homes finally remarked, "Those statues seem to be so popular in this neighborhood. Where could I get one?"

Davis now is personally associated with three of the Heismans—his own, which he presented to his alma mater, Bonita High School; one belonging to 1954 winner Alan Ameche, whose widow Glenn, himself a widower, married several years ago; and one in the family of his stepdaughter Cathy, who is married to Michael Cappelletti, brother of the 1973 winner, John Cappelletti, a running back from Penn

91

State. It was Michael and John's late brother, Joey, who was the subject of the movie *Something for Joey*.

Duty, Honor, and Country

When their West Point football careers ended, Blanchard and Davis were faced with several options—not including their commitments for active duty.

Davis had a standing offer from the Brooklyn Dodgers and Boston Red Sox to sign rich contracts, and, he admits, he dearly wanted to play major league baseball. But time was against his ambition because, he figured, he'd be nearly 10 years older than players with whom he'd have to share rookie status.

"Most players at that time came out of high school and went into the minor leagues," he said. "Those who went through that experience were in the big leagues by the time I got out of West Point. I still had at least three years of army service ahead of me, and if I then went into baseball, it would have meant some time in the minors before I moved up. It was too late in life for that, which was too bad because I really loved to play the game. It was fun. The practices were fun, and so were the games. In football, it was fun to play the games, but practices never were much fun."

Professional football desperately wanted them. In 1947, the new All-America Football Conference, just a year old, was in fierce competition for college players with the established National Football League. The Detroit Lions of the NFL drafted Davis, and the Pittsburgh Steelers drafted Blanchard. But they decided to play for the AAFC's San Francisco 49ers, which had drafted them as a team and offered each of them a $40,000 contract. That was tremendous money for that time when established stars in the NFL were making no more than $15,000.

The plan, Blanchard once explained, was for them to take a five-month leave from the service after graduation to play pro football. They would do that for three years, spending the other seven months each year on active duty. At the end of the three years, they would retire from pro football and agree to unlimited military service.

"The proposition was taken to Major General Maxwell D. Taylor, West Point's superintendent, and he bought the idea," Blanchard related. "Then the next day he called and canceled it. The military was agreeable; the politicos objected, saying, 'We are not educating boys so they can make money in football.'"

With no professional sports careers at hand, they used much of their post-graduation 60-day leave to make a movie of their careers at West Point, whose title started out as *The Big Rabble* but ended up as *The Spirit of West Point*. Davis, who had played four years at Army without any injury, badly injured his knee while making a shadow cut for the cameras during filming at UCLA's practice field. For no visible reason, his right knee buckled under him. The injury cost him an appearance later that summer in the College All-Star Game against the NFL champion Chicago Bears. Later that year, he and Blanchard were given permission by the War

Davis (No. 41) still holds the career West Point rushing record—8.3 yards per carry—more than a half century after he graduated.

Department to play in a charity All-Star game against the New York Giants. His knee again collapsed during a punt return, forcing him to have it surgically repaired.

That didn't keep him from fulfilling his three-year active duty commitment. Part of it was in South Korea in 1948 with the Fifth Regimental Combat Team, a force of 7,500 troops that was the only American military presence in the country. Davis remembers most the desolation of the country and the poverty of its people. Just three years earlier, at the end of World War II, they had been freed from 40 years of Japanese occupation.

"There was one paved road to our area from Seoul, and that city was in terrible condition," he said. "The people lived in huts made of straw or mud and covered by thatch, or in caves in the hills. The air stunk from the rice paddies and honey pots, which were containers of human waste used to fertilize the paddies. It didn't take long to realize that these people lived for one day at a time and that getting through today was a personal victory. Tomorrow would have to take care of itself."

Davis' unit had a twofold purpose: to prevent incursions by units of the Communist-led North Korean army across the 38th parallel, the political boundary separating the two Koreas; and as a token "political" force, to show the governments of South and North Korea that the United States still had an interest in the country's security.

The Americans fully knew that their survival was questionable if the 100,000-man North Korean army, well trained and fully equipped with Russian-made weapons, invaded the south. Regardless of how hard they may have fought, the South Korean army, still being organized and trained, was incapable of providing enough support to halt such an incursion. That, of course, is precisely what happened two years later when North Korea invaded South Korea and drove its army, and the few supporting American forces, to the tip of the Korean peninsula. A reinforced American army rallied in an area called the Pusan Perimeter, halted the advance, and forced the North Koreans to retreat.

Duty with the Fifth Regimental Combat Team was by no means an easy peacetime assignment. On the contrary, it became a pawn in a cold war game of global politics. The boundary line was a sieve as North Korea kept violating its prohibitions with continuous incursions into the areas patrolled by the Americans. The intention, of course, was to finally force the United States to give up and evacuate its forces. That would leave the country to the whim of the North Koreans.

"Up on the 38th parallel, whenever you went out on patrol, it was a total wartime atmosphere," Davis said. "We had to constantly check to see that no North Korean infiltrators had set up any kind of fire positions on our side of the line. When they were found, there were frequent firefights. Fortunately, I never got involved in one, but I knew some in our unit who did. We had our barracks area sprayed from time to time by machine gun fire from infiltrators, so that made us all the more vigilant and edgy."

Davis left the army after a stint as a plebe coach at West Point in 1949 and a duty tour at Ft. Monroe, in Virginia. He took his final football fling in 1950 and

1951 with two hot-and-cold seasons for the offense-happy Los Angeles Rams. He was the team's top rusher and caught 42 passes for 592 yards and four touchdowns as a rookie in 1950. The team made it to the NFL title game but lost to Cleveland, 30–28, despite his 83-yard touchdown pass on the game's first play. Davis' knee betrayed him in 1951, and his production diminished to 64 carries, a 3.1-yard average, and eight catches for 90 yards and a touchdown. Nevertheless, his contributions helped the Rams win the NFL title.

Blanchard never played pro football after that game against the Giants.

Instead, like many West Point graduates in those years, including several of his own teammates, he chose to become a pilot and began a 25-year career in what soon became the U.S. Air Force, retiring in 1971 as a brigadier general.

"The branch of service you ended up in depended on your class standing," he said. "The lower end, where I was, went to the infantry or the Army Air Corps, and 25 percent of us in that group were not interested in walking. So, I went off to Randolph Field in San Antonio to begin primary training. I did AT-6 prop planes, then P-51s and then F-80 and F-84 jet fighters."

Six months before the Korean War started, Blanchard was assigned to the 57th Fighter Group of the 64th Fighter Interceptor Squadron, near Anchorage, Alaska. It was the nation's first line of defense if the Russians ever sent their bombers across the Siberian Sea. It was a touchy time, with plenty of two-a-day training missions, alerts, and constant vigils, and it got even touchier once the war in Korea began.

Following two coaching stints at West Point under Blaik, sandwiched around a duty tour as an instructor in all-weather flying at Tandall Field, in Panama City, he was sent to England. In the spring of 1959, Blanchard, then a major in the air force, was cited for bravery for safely riding his burning jet fighter to the ground rather than risking a crash into the English village of Fincingfield. It was adjacent to the air force base at Wethersfield, England, where he was operations officer of the 77th Tactical Fighter Squadron of the Third Air Force.

Blanchard was shooting an approach in hazy and foggy conditions. He glanced at his instrument panel and saw that his oil pressure gauge read "0."

"The next thing I know, a big red light came on, and it read 'FIRE,'" Blanchard said. "The control tower confirmed that it could see that my plane was smoking, and then I saw the smoke in my rearview mirror.

"I had two choices, jump out or land. The bail-out system was automatic but not as comforting. All of this took about 10 minutes, and there was no debating what I would do. The village of Fincingfield was straight ahead, and the plane might have hit either the village or the other heavily populated areas. According to the emergency procedures, I was supposed to land the plane if it has power, and I still was under power. I just hoped I'd keep the plane running until I got on the ground. It stayed alive, so I just landed the plane, shut down the engine, and jumped out."

He received worldwide notoriety for that action, but his reaction then and now was very basic: it was just something that had to be done, and he did it. He has never dwelt on the subject of doing valorous deeds, though he spent a year in harm's way

95

Blanchard (right) saw action as a fighter pilot during his long and distinguished military career.

while flying 113 missions during the Vietnam War. He once said that he grew up without having any heroes in his life, though there is no doubt that "Big Doc" has always filled that role.

When he was at West Point as a cadet, one of his tactical officers, John Corley, had won the Distinguished Service Cross, five Silver Stars, the Legion of Merit, the Soldier's Medal, four Bronze Stars, and the Purple Heart during three years of combat in Africa and Europe. He went to Korea with the 24th Division and won another Distinguished Service Cross, three more Silver Stars, and another Legion of Merit, as well as a battlefield promotion to colonel.

"Like a lot of people who do reckless things in the heat of battle, he was a bit crazy," Blanchard said. "He graduated from West Point in 1938, washed out as an air cadet, and was assigned to the infantry. One of his more heroic deeds was charging a German machine-gun nest and wiping it out with a handful of grenades.

"Why would somebody do something like that? Most guys are scared to death in battle, and if they're brave beyond what is reasonable behavior, then they're also a bit crazy. No one who's ever fought in a war considered it fun, but more often than not, in battle you have to do something or else you'll get yourself killed just standing around.

"One of the truly heroic fighter pilots I knew was General Jay Robbins, who I worked with in England and later in Austin, Texas, with the 12th Air Force. During World War II, he flew a P-38. He played football at Texas A&M, and he talked more about that than he did about his wartime experiences. But I found out that he shot down 22 enemy planes and was one of our leading World War II aces."

Several months after the Wethersfield incident, Blanchard was given command of the squadron until 1962, when he was assigned to the Air Force Academy as the plebe coach under head coach Ben Martin. When his old teammate Ed Rafalko became the Academy's athletic director, he made Blanchard his assistant until 1968 when Blanchard was sent to Thailand as wing operations director of the 388th Tactical Fighter Wing. He flew F-105 fighter-bombers, and 84 of his 113 combat missions were over North Vietnam.

"We never had any air-to-air combat missions," he said. "We attacked their supply routes and military positions and dropped some bombs. When we did that, it was like, 'Oops, there goes another Cadillac,' because that was the cost of the armament."

Blanchard had followed a well-worn path to active duty, one taken nearly two decades earlier by "Light Horse" Harry Wilson, half of the celebrated and afore-mentioned Wilson-Cagle backfield tandem which, like Blanchard and Davis, is enshrined in College Football's Hall of Fame. Wilson chose the army air corps after graduation, and during World War II, he distinguished himself as commander of the 42nd Medium Bomber Group of the 13th Air Force in the Pacific, where he was awarded the Distinguished Flying Cross and seven Air Medals.

Wilson was joined in the air corps during the war by some of Blaik's other eager young players from the early forties, including Robin Olds, a guard, and

97

running backs Jim Watkins and Hank Mazur. In addition to their regular studies at West Point, they took flight instruction at nearby Stewart Field. After graduation, they were sent immediately to advanced flight training, and then to air corps units around the world. That entire group ran the gamut of military aviation during their careers, starting in fast propeller-driven fighter planes and finishing in the cockpits of the air force's latest jets.

Watkins joined the 483rd Bomber Group of the 15th Air Force in the Mediterranean theater of operations and won two Distinguished Flying Crosses and five Air Medals. Mazur became a flight leader and squadron commander of the 368th Fighter Group and was awarded two Distinguished Flying Crosses and seventeen

98

General Robin Olds became one of the air force's most decorated pilots.

USMA Library Special Collections and Archives Division

Air Medals. Olds' exploits as a fighter pilot earned him two Silver Stars, two Distinguished Flying Crosses, and twenty-eight Air Medals.

"I almost didn't get overseas," said Olds, a retired air force brigadier general and one of its most decorated pilots. "There were some screwy rules in place at the time about who would go overseas, so seven of us who were training in P-38s in California went into Los Angeles and told the sergeant at the headquarters that we wanted to go.

"'You mean you want to go to war?' he asked us, a bit incredulously."

Olds flew one tour of 25 missions in Europe, came home for a few weeks' rest, and then finished the war with the 434th Fighter Squadron, logging 107 missions during which he shot down 13 German planes and destroyed another 111 on the ground while flying P-138s and P-51s. When the war ended, he had been awarded two Silver Stars, two Distinguished Flying Crosses, and twenty-eight Air Medals.

"There were 40 men in our squadron, and you moved up by attrition and proficiency," he said. "Air battles took the greatest toll, and before I was finished over there, I was the squadron commander with the rank of major, and I was only 23."

He flew in combat again in Vietnam as commander of the Eighth Tactical Fighter Wing, earning the Air Force Cross, two more Silver Stars, the Legion of Merit, four Distinguished Flying Crosses, and twelve Air Medals. Total medal count: six Distinguished Flying Crosses, four Silver Stars, forty Air Medals, one Legion of Merit, and one Air Force Cross.

99

Olds, as was the case with nearly every former football player who was a fighter pilot—in the army and the navy—played football with the same verve and spirit as he flew fighter planes. It was all out and with the same intent of burying an opponent. That is why he was an All-American tackle in 1942. He was inducted into the College Football Hall of Fame in 1985.

He also remembers an Army-Navy game in 1942, at the Naval Academy, when a flying elbow cost him his teeth. "I was crawling around looking for my teeth, and then I said to [teammate] Frank Merritt, 'What will I do with them if I find them?'

"The doctor took me into the locker room, and it took 32 stitches to sew up my mouth. When I came back, I told Colonel Blaik that I wanted to go back into the game.

"'Can he do that?' Blaik asked the doctor.

"'He can if he wants to,' the doctor replied. So I went in, and it took me three plays to get the guy who knocked out my teeth."

The battlefield tradition continued with Blanchard's own teammates. The aforementioned Ed Rafalko, an end on the 1944 team who is now a retired air force major general, won the Legion of Merit and six Air Medals while flying in Vietnam as vice commander of the Strategic Air Command's 4258th Strategic Wing, based in Thailand. He flew more than 120 missions, often leading three dozen B-52s "wherever [General] Creighton Abrams wanted us to bomb."

"We had some interesting missions when we got over North Vietnam," he admitted, "dodging SA-2s [communist ground-to-air missiles, called SAMs]. They got your attention, and soon you recalled everything the briefers told you before you took off."

When he returned from his morning bombing runs, he'd go over to another part of the giant air force base and command a group of tanker planes for afternoon missions that refueled smaller air force bombers.

Jim Enos, a member of the Blanchard-Davis teams for three years, was stationed at the headquarters of the Fifth Air Force in Japan in 1950, working directly for its vice commander, Lieutenant General Edward J. Timberlake Jr. Timberlake's father had been a starter on the first football team ever fielded by West Point in 1890.

Enos had flown World War II vintage, propeller-driven A-26 bombers before that assignment and immediately volunteered to fly the planes in combat missions over Korea. "General Timberlake wrote me orders in longhand, dispatching me to Korea, and I flew 75 missions, mostly in support of army ground forces," he recalled. "I collected a few holes in my plane from ground fire, but I was fortunate in not getting shot down because some in our group did. In addition to going after targets of opportunity and being assigned to area targets—that was boring because you were controlled by someone on the ground—we did a lot of night strafing and bombing. It was always a petrifying experience."

His work earned him the Distinguished Flying Cross and seven Air Medals. More than a decade later, he crossed paths with Blanchard for a night of reliving old times. Both were flying jet aircraft from bases in Thailand, Enos as deputy commander of the 15th Tactical Fighter Wing. Like Blanchard, his 100 missions were primarily concerned with bombing and strafing, and no air-to-air combat.

The heroic action was not limited to air force members, either.

Two former Army team captains, guard Joe Steffy in 1947 and end John Trent in 1950, were members of the same class at the Infantry School at Ft. Benning, Georgia, in 1950. Steffy and Trent joined the Third Division in North Korea as it was fighting for its life trying to escape an ambush by a huge Chinese Communist army.

"One of the saddest days of my life was burying John on a snowy hillside near Wonson, North Korea, on November 15, 1950," Steffy said. "I'll never forget the date. It was a bitter cold, snowy day. He had been there just a week when he was killed in action. Seven months earlier, he was the best man at my wedding."

A few days later, Steffy won a Purple Heart during a fierce battle that helped thousands of American troops to escape annihilation and be evacuated from the North Korean port of Hungnam. The following spring, he won a Silver Star for heroism in a battle that ultimately entrapped hundreds of enemy troops attempting to flee their positions near Ouijongbu, northwest of Seoul.

Three other linemen who played on all the Blanchard and Davis teams— guards Sheldon Biles and Art Gerometta, and Fuson—distinguished themselves in battle. Biles, who, as an adviser to South Vietnamese forces in 1968–1969, was always heavily involved in combat operations, won the Legion of Merit and the Bronze Star. Fuson commanded one of the first groups of American forces in the Seventh Cavalry Regiment to enter the Korean War, and he earned the Purple Heart and Bronze Star with "V."

In one of the freak turns that often govern a soldier's fate, Gerometta was in a group of six officers who had reported to the U.S. Army's Camp Drake Replacement Center near Tokyo, en route to the First Cavalry Division in Korea. The group was unaccountably split up, three of the officers going to Korea on one day and Gerometta and two others going the next day. When Gerometta's group arrived, it learned that the first trio was killed soon after joining their unit. Gerometta later won the Silver Star, Bronze Star, Combat Infantryman's Badge, and a Purple Heart.

There was a spirit of unselfishness among all of those men that is the very essence of the word *valor*, and it was at the core of what they did for their football teams and in serving their country. That same spirit moved Blanchard, four months after he retired from the air force after logging more than 5,000 hours of flying time, to take an appointment for several years as commandant of cadets at New Mexico Military Institute (NMMI). A decade earlier, the school had as one of its students a young quarterback name Roger Staubach, enrolled to prepare for admittance to the Naval Academy, where he enjoyed some of his greatest football moments against Blanchard's alma mater.

Blanchard and his late wife, Jody, had bought a home in Burnet, Texas, not far from Austin (and just 13 miles from Oatmeal), where he had been assigned to 12th Air Force headquarters prior to retirement. That small, picturesque community was an ideal location for someone like Blanchard, who loved the outdoors, particularly anyplace where he could cast a line and catch a fish. It sat amidst several park areas with lakes and streams and was such a perfect spot that they decided to live there full-time.

His first four months in retirement were an idyllic time, but there was still something inside of him that he needed to give back. It became more important than a much-deserved life of leisure for someone who had done so much for his country. His association with football as a player, during two coaching assignments at West Point under Blaik, and as a plebe coach and assistant athletic director for four years at the Air Force Academy had constructed a package of experiences that he believed could help shape the lives and careers of the young cadets at NMMI.

"Association with football establishes a set of values for youth which determine their living patterns," he said. "I always liked working with young people, and I had considered a career in coaching. But you can't be in the service and be a full-time coach at the same time and still maintain the proper career progression. So, I made the decision to remain in the air force, and it was the right decision for me. When you have a job you enjoy doing, you don't throw it away.

"But when my air force career ended, I had the opportunity to pursue those other avenues, and I did it."

Art Gerometta.

Davis once had an opportunity to help a friend in crisis, and in the same spirit of unselfishness, he came through with flying colors.

While he was serving as an assistant coach at West Point in the late forties, the wife of West Point sports publicity director Joe Cahill was suddenly afflicted with infantile paralysis and rushed to a hospital where she died three days later. During the emergency, Davis watched over the Cahills' seven-year-old son, all the while ignoring the warnings that he, too, could become infected with the disease.

Unlike his feats on a football field, his Heisman Trophy, and myriad records, few inside or outside West Point ever knew of this valorous deed. That was as he wished, just as those who were influenced by Doc Blanchard as players and students at the Air Force Academy and New Mexico Military Institute are the only ones who really know what he did for them.

It was all part of being Mr. Inside and Mr. Outside.

103

Chapter 3
Pete Dawkins

Early in 1966, during the gradual escalation of American involvement in the civil war that was raging in South Vietnam, one of those unpredictable things that so often happen on a battlefield befell the elite First Airborne Battalion of South Vietnam's army, and Company F, Second Battalion, Seventh U.S. Marines. They suddenly became embroiled in a bitter battle against overwhelming forces from North Vietnam's army.

The First Airborne Battalion had arrived at the battle site aboard helicopters and was able to get a minimal number of forces on the ground before the North Vietnamese began shooting down the choppers. This wasn't how the operation had been planned, but like most battles, preplanning can quickly disintegrate into almost catch-as-catch-can affairs where individual leadership and the ability to correctly analyze and react to a suddenly changed situation will carry the day, or at least stave off disaster.

Averting disaster was one role of United States Army officers like Major Pete Dawkins, who served as senior advisers to the South Vietnamese army.

Dawkins was assigned to this crack unit, and he suddenly found himself trying to make sense of the mayhem that was unfolding around him. The battalion was disorganized, outnumbered, and almost bereft of tactical integrity because it had become a hybrid unit, half South Vietnamese troops and half marines.

To make matters worse, the commanders of the South Vietnamese troops had lost control of the situation, so it was left to Dawkins to do what he had always done best—he stepped up, took command, and then worked to restore order to his battle line. He controlled the South Vietnamese forces by directing them in their own language, a recently learned skill from a four-month assignment at the Defense Language Institute at the Presidio in Monterey, California, and one that he had improved upon since his arrival in Vietnam the previous September. Next, he had to switch frequencies on his command radios and use English to integrate the marines and air cover until the latter was deterred by bad weather. His situation was greatly strengthened by withering fire from marine artillerymen who poured a continuous barrage into the enemy concentrations and helped to break up their repeated attacks.

It was nearly midnight when he received a call from the commander of the marine artillery unit saying that his unit had just about exhausted its ammunition and would soon have to cease the supporting fire.

"We were in an extreme state," Dawkins said. "We were outnumbered, surrounded, cut off, and unable to get in reinforcements. Worse still, our positions were at the base of a hill and the enemy was atop it, rolling down grenades and firing mortars easily onto our positions. We were getting chewed up and suffering a lot of casualties.

"When the artillery commander told me they were out of ammunition and would soon have to cease their support, I said, 'The only thing keeping us alive is your support, and if you can't keep it up, then we're not going to make it.' He said he understood but there was nothing he could do because our rules forbade resupply over unsecured roads during darkness, and the only road between him and the supply base was unsecured.

"Neither of us realized it, but Joe Platt, a recently promoted marine brigadier, overheard our conversation on his radio. He had been a commissioned officer since 1940, and this was his third major war. In fact, I found out later that he had served on Guadalcanal in the Solomon Islands in 1942, when my dad was there with the marines.

"I never had the privilege of meeting General Platt, but he evidently said to himself, 'To hell with the rules,' and on his own, he ordered a convoy of trucks to be loaded with 155-mm ammunition and sent down that unsecured road, in the dark, to resupply the batteries. We also knew two things: the North Vietnamese had also monitored the conversation and believed we'd be easy pickings without the artillery support, and we knew that when the artillery fire stopped, they would launch an attack just before dawn.

"That's exactly when they staged a massive attack, and the marine batteries, with that fresh ammunition, just cut them apart and saved our lives. But had it not been for Brigadier Joe Platt putting his marines in harm's way, to meet a need desperately required, my name would be among those engraved on that solemn black granite monument to those killed in action in Vietnam that is such a special part of the Mall in Washington. I still think about him nearly every day."

Of course, that was the same Pete Dawkins who, in the fall of 1958, went from a relatively unknown Army halfback to the most recognizable college football player in the nation. In so doing, he also was a unanimous All-America selection and a most improbable recipient of the Heisman Trophy, capping, as he has so aptly put it, "an all-time Cinderella season on an all-time Cinderella team."

For the previous two years, he was best known to Army fans only for being a very workmanlike player. In 1956, he didn't play enough to earn a varsity letter, and in 1957, he was a starter but had played in the shadow of Bob Anderson, a sophomore from Miami, Florida, who was a more talented and spectacular runner.

All of that changed in 1958. When that season ended, an entire nation soon discovered what those who lived within the boundaries of West Point had long known about this young cadet from Royal Oak, Michigan. Their regard for Dawkins was almost godlike because he seemed capable of doing anything he wished including, some proclaimed, walking across the Hudson River from its west bank below the U.S. Military Academy's mighty ramparts to the east side, where he could peer back into Michie Stadium, home of Army's football team.

Pete Dawkins electrified the nation as a running back for the Cadets in his Heisman Trophy–winning season of 1958.

Downtown Athletic Club

That year, at age 20, Dawkins was the first captain of the Corps of Cadets, the highest honor and most important position that a cadet could hold. He meted out justice and enforced discipline to the nearly 2,500 cadets who made up the corps at that time. He presided over elaborate rituals and officially welcomed all visiting dignitaries.

On ceremonial occasions such as the weekly formal parades across the famed Plain, his uniform was emblazoned with six stripes on his sleeves and a tall plume on his hat. Whenever he barked orders on these occasions, they were carried out by two regimental commanders, six battalion commanders, and twenty-four company commanders.

The second highest honor at West Point was to be captain of the football team. Dawkins' teammates had recognized his influence on them and elected him their captain. In football, the quality of leadership is never more apparent than in a team setting. A necessity for a successful team is to have one of its members help to channel the emotions and actions of the players.

"This is particularly true at West Point, where there is an ingrained sense of the chain of command, of hierarchies, and more of a leadership responsibility being captain of the football team," Dawkins said. "Yet, I didn't consciously try to assert leadership. It came in a natural way because my teammates looked to me at certain moments to establish a mood or a spirit. I felt that responsibility, and I worried at times whether I was living up to it.

"The environment at West Point makes it easier. You didn't have to force your way in because there was a natural receptivity. We had a lot of leaders on that team, really a whole team of leaders because West Point is like a leadership laboratory. It could have turned very dysfunctional if everyone competed to be captain, but that never happened. It was a very positive part of that spirit of that team—one of the secrets of our success that year."

That 1958 Army football team was undefeated in nine games, winning eight and tying the other, en route to being ranked third in the nation and winning the prestigious Lambert Trophy, emblematic of the Eastern championship.

Third in individual importance at West Point was the job as class president. You guessed it. Dawkins was president of the class of 1959.

The only other honor at West Point was given to "star men," and they comprised the top academic 5 percent of each class. In his class of 503 who started 1958 as seniors, Dawkins ranked seventh, and thus he was also a member of that elite group. At graduation 10 months later, Dawkins ranked 10th in a class of 498.

To place all of this in perspective, in the 156-year history of West Point, to 1958, only 53 first captains had been "star men"; only 11 first captains had been class presidents; only 2 first captains had been football captains.

Dawkins was the first cadet ever to hold all four distinctions in one year.

The manner in which he was able to juggle those four prestigious positions gave a tremendous insight into how he would also manage a career that at one point

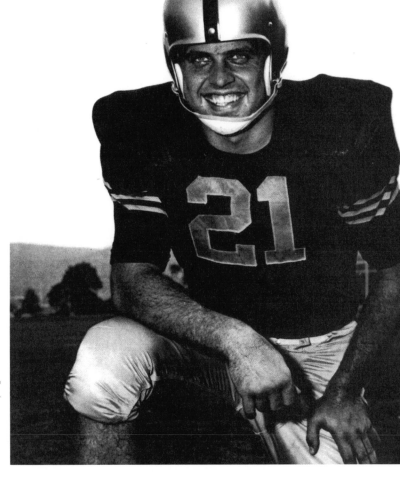

In 1957 Dawkins had played in the shadow of Bob Anderson.

saw him become the youngest brigadier general on the army's active duty rolls in 1981.

"Looking back, that entire senior year was wonderful, and no one could have wished for anything more," he said. "It was a fantasy of delight in an atmosphere that was a rampage of activity, from dawn to taps every day. But it also was very hard. During the football season, I had a full load of classes, no telescoped schedules as in civilian colleges. In the latter half of the season, like everyone else on the team, I was physically beaten up, chronically tired, and not getting all of my studying accomplished.

"But I had a kind of 'study team,' a group of friends who would brief me on an upcoming class while we were taking the seven or ten minutes to walk to it. They told me what I should have read and really got me through on those briefings. There never was anything that would clash with the Academy's honor code by giving exam questions and answers. In fact, what sometimes got them annoyed at me was my getting a higher grade on the tests than they did."

Dawkins survived that madcap schedule largely because of West Point's built-in time-management techniques, an asset he uses to this day. "They have always benefited me, inside and outside the military," he said. "I don't know how I could have survived that senior year without them."

Less than a decade later, Dawkins also became one of America's first military heroes in its early military involvement in Vietnam. From time to time in 1965–1966, while he was on his lone combat tour, journalists covering the war rekindled the fame he had enjoyed as a Heisman Trophy winner. In so doing, that unforgettable 1958 season, neatly put away in the history books, was reawakened, and so was the almost unbelievable sequence of events that had made him one of the most unique Heisman Trophy winners of all time.

His lack of notoriety at the start of the 1958 season is in part because life at the Military Academy was then an almost hermetically sealed existence. The public's only view generally came at football games at Michie Stadium in the fall when thousands of visitors trekked onto the post and gawked as much at the majestic gray stone buildings as at the gray-clad cadets.

In mid-October, the gray-on-gray was broken up with breathtaking splashes of autumnal colors spread throughout the entire Academy. They ran up and down the streets and roads that curved through the hills of this unique military community, and they were spread in every direction from atop the Academy's ramparts through the scenic Hudson River Valley.

As part of the unique football experience that is a game at West Point, there were elaborate tailgate luncheons with tables covered with linen cloths and napkins upon which sat fine china and silver, and even candelabra. Lunch in this unique setting really was a transformation of a five-star restaurant. When it was finished, everyone moved into what was then a very modest 28,000-seat stadium named for Dennis Michie, the founder of Army's football program.

For the next three hours, the Corps of Cadets roared its collective throat raw with raspy cheering for its team. Cannons roared a salute when the Army team first appeared, they were fired every time it scored, and at the end of the game there was a final salute to the efforts its football warriors had expended that day. Their roars echoed and reechoed as they cascaded down the Hudson Valley, bouncing off the granite walls that shot tall and straight from the riverbed to the west of the post, skipping over the waters of the Hudson River as it headed upstate toward Albany or downstate toward the canyons of New York City, and bounding into the rolling hills to the east. The post band lustily played "On Brave Old Army Team" every time the Cadets scored, accompanied by the even lustier voices of 2,400 cadets and thousands

Dennis Michie.

of Army's very loyal football fans. Throughout the afternoon, young men very deftly rode the three famed Army mule mascots up and down the sidelines, further engendering a spirit and emotion unique to Army football.

When the afternoon ended, the throngs would leave, and West Point would revert to that hermetically sealed state. Cadets and regular army personnel assigned to the post quietly resumed their very structured routines, all of them anonymous persons until some time, long after they had left the Plain, they might be called into a conflict that would bring alive their motto of Duty, Honor, and Country.

Earl "Red" Blaik.

In the fall of 1958, the anonymous state that governed the lives of Army's football team was suddenly lifted. It began in the season's first game when that Army team shook up the college football world by unveiling a new, unique system it called the Lonely End Offense. It was a revolutionary, albeit short-lived, alignment in which a 6'2" junior end named Bill Carpenter became celebrated for never once entering his team's offensive huddle during that entire season. Instead, he stood about 15–18 yards away while his 10 teammates gathered around quarterback Joe Caldwell and listened to him call every play.

This unconventional strategy was the brainchild of Army's legendary head coach, Earl "Red" Blaik. The process began during post-1957 season film study when Blaik found that his team did not have the depth to physically compete game after game against bigger, more powerful teams and had worn down in the second half. Opposing outside linebackers and cornerbacks were successfully jamming the Cadets' rushing offense. What was needed, given the limitations of his team's talent and depth, was something that would spread those defenses and lessen their pressure.

Enter the Lonely End.

He selected Carpenter, a relatively unknown player who had missed his entire sophomore season after a nonfootball injury, because he had shown during his plebe year that he was a superb receiver. He had sufficient speed to get open downfield and catch the football, and he was a tenacious blocker and defensive player.

113

Blaik installed this offense, later called the Lonely End Formation, in spring drills. In the original version, Carpenter wasn't "lonely" because he entered and left the huddle on every play and stationed himself 15 yards outside the closest offensive lineman to his position. At the College All-Star Game in Chicago that summer, Blaik outlined the concept to one of his former assistants, Andy Gustafson, then head coach at the University of Miami. Gustafson pointed out that moving the end in and out of the huddle and flanking him 15 yards on every offensive play would exhaust him long before the game ended.

"He was right," Carpenter said later. "Until they decided to hold me out of the huddle, I was more of a tired end than a lonely one."

When preseason practice began, Blaik permanently stationed the Lonely End 15 yards outside the tackle, usually on the right side of the field. For an entire season, as Army racked up one victory after another, the entire country, as well as its opponents, tried to figure out how Carpenter knew what play was being run, particularly when many involved the ball being thrown to him. It wasn't until six weeks after the season ended that Blaik finally revealed the secrets—on the same night, incidentally, that he astounded a huge crowd attending the Lambert Trophy awards banquet in New York City by announcing that he was retiring after 18 seasons as Army's football coach.

"He got each play by watching the quarterback's foot movements," Blaik explained to the stunned audience. "If he stood in the huddle with his feet squared, the play was a run. If either foot was advanced, it was a pass. Dawkins was always stationed at the end of the huddle closest to Carpenter, and as he left it to line up,

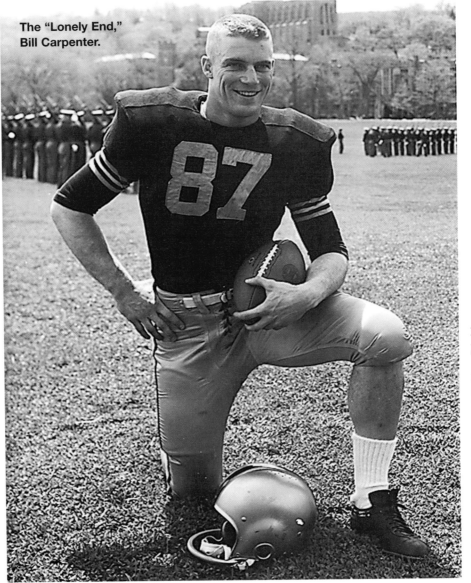

The "Lonely End," Bill Carpenter.

USMA Library Special Collections and Archives Division

he sent a signal indicating which of the five designated routes would be used on that play. Carpenter ran those routes, whether it be as a downfield blocker on a running play, or if he was a potential receiver on a pass play.

"Regardless of the play, the defense still had to station a player near him on every down, and that loosened their alignment and gave us more room to run our offense."

"It was a triumph of geometry to give us a half-man advantage because no one could cover Bill man-for-man," Dawkins said. "The logic was to make defenses cover him as a flanker, thereby forcing a lineman to move out wider, breaking up the defensive front. If the front remained steady and the safety covered the flanker, rotation of the entire secondary was necessary for deep coverage of the flanker, or Lonely End."

Carpenter worked the concept to perfection, and after two record-setting seasons, Blaik called him the best end in West Point football history. Blaik loved his tenacity as a blocker and tackler as much as his receiving ability. He caught 22 passes for 453 yards in 1958, and in 1959 he had a record-setting 43 receptions for 591 yards. "There would have been no Lonely End if there had been no Carpenter," Blaik said.

Later, the "Lonely End" tag was changed by the media to become the "Lonesome End." That was the name later given by Carpenter to his home in northern Montana. Blaik never recognized "Lonesome," calling it "mawkish," while "Lonely," he said, implied a "dignified stoicism."

That Lonely End and Dawkins flashed into national prominence in the opening game of the 1958 season with an astounding 45–8 victory over favored South Carolina. Dawkins scored four touchdowns, and a blizzard of questions descended upon Army's team demanding to know more about its new offense and the sudden emergence of Dawkins as an offensive force.

115

It wasn't long before Dawkins became the most celebrated Army football player since two other Heisman Trophy winners, Felix "Doc" Blanchard and Glenn Davis, were college football's most dominating players in the mid-forties. All that he achieved as a cadet was put on public display, and as more and more scrutiny was given to his football skills, he also began to emerge as someone fresh and different from the usual profile of a college football player.

It certainly helped that West Point was covered by the huge media machine that inhabited the New York City metropolitan area's 12 million population center, located just an hour away. It was rightly called the "media capital of the world" because within that area there were a dozen and a half daily newspapers, and many of those had national influence. In addition, the two major domestic wire services, several newspaper features syndicates, all the big-circulation weekly magazines of that time, plus the rapidly growing television and radio industries churned out millions of words and pictures daily. Anything that happened within their purview instantly became bigger than life.

Dawkins was soon included in that roundup, and the media began a steady trek to the Military Academy, seeking to find out about him and more about that unique Army team and its new offense. At that time, most within that media brigade were longtime sportswriters and columnists, hard-bitten, crusty, and often cynical about the intellectual depths of young college players. Dawkins delighted them because he dispensed what many considered extraordinary wisdom, poise, and bearing for someone so young. After an interview session, most of the media's cynicism

Downtown Athletic Club

Whether or not he was stopped on this play,
it usually took more than one defender to
bring down Dawkins.

FIELD OF VALOR

soon melted, and they also became believers . . . wave after wave conceding that yes, it was absolutely possible for someone so young to be so self-assured, so impressive, and to have the acumen of someone thrice his age. Though it was never Dawkins' intent, he had those old firebrands singing his praises in print and on the air as if there had never been a college football player quite like him.

Blaik also played a very significant role in this phenomenon, one that really played a large part in helping Dawkins to win the Heisman Trophy. Blaik had a hammerlock on all the influential New York City football writers, and anything he ever said or did had the authority of almost papal significance. That summer, during his annual hiatus with several of his sportswriter friends at his Bull Pond compound near West Point, he unveiled his new alignment. Stanley Woodward, sports editor of the *New York Herald-Tribune*, a Blaik confidant considered the leading college football writer in the East at that time, looked at the plan and said, "You ought to call it the Lonely End attack." Woodward unveiled the "Lonely End" tag in his column the day after Blaik had introduced it in his team's stunning opening game victory.

"He was a powerful, astoundingly potent leader," Dawkins said of Blaik. "We all drew strength from him. He was by manner aloof. He was not a shouter. He was stern and an absolutely no-nonsense man.

"Yet, he had this magical quality, possessed by all great coaches, that he made you want to win, to do well, not for your own glory, but because you had a responsibility to play at your very best all the time. He was expecting you to do just that. If not, then you felt you were disappointing him. That's a potent kind of leadership because he put it on your shoulders. If you had any pride, you didn't want to let him down. He was a master of tapping into the wellspring of that feeling."

Bob Anderson believed that Blaik's role with the players on that team has never been fully appreciated other than for his development of the Lonely End offense. "He had such a great effect on each individual," he said. "He was someone who I'd run through a wall for if he asked me, and not worry about why he wanted me to do it. We enjoyed playing for him, and it really showed that season."

Blaik produced such strong feelings despite the huge differences between the lives of football players in a civilian school and those who attended the Military Academy. The latter had specifically dedicated themselves to learning how to defend their country while playing football, and they were a continuing example of General Douglas MacArthur's feelings about the role of football in the preparation of cadets to serve their country.

"It's unique," he said of the West Point football experience. "West Point without the Army football team just wouldn't be West Point. Probably, more than at any college in America the whole essence of the place is reflected in sports in general, but in the Army football team in particular. The Military Academy is really built around the spirit of winning and victory. Competition is the daily fare of the place. The will to win and the competitiveness and all of the features of athletics are wedded to the purpose of the place, and the Army football team becomes a metaphor for

Dawkins was
captain of the
undefeated 1958
Army team that
won the Lambert
Trophy, given at
that time to
the Eastern
Champion.

118

Downtown Athletic Club

the purpose of the Academy. In a very real and vivid way, football symbolizes the spirit of West Point."

Dawkins, like all football players before him and since his departure, was well aware of the twin traditions of football on the playing field and war on the battlefield. They had to look no further than the life of cadet Dennis Mahan Michie, the father of Army football. He was killed in the Battle of San Juan Hill during the Spanish-American War, just nine years after he had founded Army's football program in a one-game season against Navy in 1890.

That very brief season lasted for 90 minutes, and Navy won 24–0. But more important, it marked the beginning of two great football traditions—Army football and the Army-Navy game.

Nearly 70 years later, Dawkins was an integral part of that football tradition; and it wasn't too long until he also became part of the tradition's other side, heroism on the battlefield. What that meant was never so forcibly demonstrated than during World War II when General George C. Marshall, the army's chief of staff, sent out the order: "I have a secret and dangerous mission. Send me an Army football player." He got his man, whose name never was revealed because the "secret and dangerous mission" was scrubbed. But the bar was set.

As noted earlier in this book, General of the Armies Dwight D. Eisenhower, the supreme Allied commander during the invasion and liberation of western Europe in World War II, was a halfback on the 1912 team, who reluctantly gave up the sport because of a knee injury in a game that season against Tufts. One of his proudest moments occurred earlier when he stopped Carlisle's great Jim Thorpe with a head-on tackle. He told Blaik in 1958 that he was lured to West Point in 1911 by the prospect of playing football, and after the knee injury ended his career, he was so despondent that he almost resigned. But Army coach Charley Daly asked him to help coach the "B" squad and it renewed his spirit to stay and graduate.

Not only did great leaders like Eisenhower and MacArthur direct victory in World War II, but many of their subordinate commanders had been football

119

Arthur Corr/D.A.C.

Pete Dawkins with two other Heisman winners: Gary Beban, UCLA (1967) and Paul Hornung, Notre Dame (1956).

players. Two of them were members of Army teams in the mid-twenties, Tom Trapnell and Maurice Daly. They were together in the Philippines when, shortly after Pearl Harbor was attacked, the Japanese invaded the main island of Luzon where most of the U.S. forces were stationed under MacArthur's command. Daly, a member of the Army Air Corps, was forced to organize a provisional battalion of mechanics, pilots, radio operators, and other personnel at Clark Field after the Japanese destroyed American air power early in the battle.

During one battle, he called his commanding officer and recommended a withdrawal, reporting the Japanese forces within sight.

"How far away from your position are they?" he was asked.

"About 10 yards," came the noncommittal reply.

Maurice Daly.

Both were heroes, and Daly proved to be an inspiration to the thousands of American prisoners of war forced to share with him the starvation and privation of the Bataan Death March. The men were deliberately marched, without rest, during the torrid tropical heat and allowed to drink only from muddy pools. Daly rallied his men's fallen spirits daily and kept them alive and moving. But one day, his jovial manner disappeared after a Japanese guard cracked his skull with a rifle butt while he protected three of his men who had broken ranks and ran to slake their unbearable thirst from a well.

Then, it became a bitter battle of wills between Daly and his captors. He was unrelenting in badgering the Japanese prison camp guards to provide more for his men. He feared none of them, and periodically he stalked into the camp commander's office to present a list of demands for better living conditions. When Daly finished delivering the list, he then proceeded to tell the commander what he thought of his camp, the conditions that existed, the man himself, and his honorable ancestors. The prison camp commander so feared Daly that he never talked to him unless a guard, with rifle and fixed bayonet at the ready, was standing next to him.

121

Late in 1944, when American forces started to liberate the Philippines, the Japanese decided to send U.S. prisoners to Japan or to the Asian mainland. Trapnell and Daly were put aboard the *Oryoku Maru* in Subic Bay with 1,500 other POWs. Before it got underway, the ship, unmarked as a POW carrier, was bombed by U.S. planes, which mistook it for a Japanese cargo ship. Only half of the prisoners escaped death from the raid. Many of the survivors were wounded, and they were all sent temporarily to a nearby prison camp where more died. Those survivors, which included Daly and Trapnell, were then placed on board another unmarked POW carrier, *Enoura Maru*. When it reached Formosa, it also was attacked by U.S. planes whose pilots were unaware of the human cargo. Again, more prisoners were killed or wounded, but the survivors, including Daly and Trapnell, were placed on a third ship, *Brazil Maru*, and sailed for Japan. The trip was made in January. The winter weather was severe, and food and shelter were almost nonexistent.

One night Daly and Trapnell, who had shared all of the battles, the privations, and the sinkings, huddled under a light blanket and tried to sleep. When Trapnell awoke the next morning, Daly lay cold next to him. He had paid the price on the football field and on the battlefield.

When Dawkins was enjoying such great personal success during the 1958 season, he also was being compared to MacArthur, Eisenhower, Marshall, and other famous American military leaders. Even his fellow cadets, in their own kidding way, recognized his great potential.

"If Dawkins had been at the Academy when Douglas MacArthur was superintendent, the general would have made a fine aide for Pete!" was one version of their recognition.

When he was presented with the Maxwell Award as the nation's outstanding college player in 1958, West Point's commandant of cadets at the time, Brigadier General John L. Throckmorton, told the hundreds who had gathered to honor him,

General Douglas MacArthur.

AP/Wide World Photos

"Mr. Dawkins has taken full advantage of everything West Point has to offer . . . the will to succeed and the desire to excel—these Mr. Dawkins has."

Assistant coach Tom Harp put it in football terms for that same audience: "In all things, the corps felt as the coaches did, 'Just give the ball to Pete and everything will be alright.'"

In the seventies, when Dawkins was a major and assigned to West Point as an instructor, he occasionally helped the football team as an assistant coach. He ran wind sprints with the players, "and often beat most of 'em," head coach Tom Cahill said at the time. "His impact on the cadets personifies what they're supposed to be someday."

Blaik even went so far as to predict that he would eventually become the army's chief of staff, the highest post for an army officer. So impressive was this young native of Michigan, no one demurred in that prediction because Blaik was never given to excessive hyperbole when discussing the career projections for any of his players.

Three years before, when Dawkins was a plebe, such notoriety would have been considered impossible. He was reluctantly accepted at West Point, by its academic counselors and by Blaik, and the success that he achieved was without a doubt an exercise in personal courage and conviction because he had to overcome some very stiff obstacles to first gain entry and then to succeed as an athlete.

123

He came to West Point from Cranbrook Prep in Bloomfield Hills, Michigan, where he was a 110-pound left-handed quarterback and a much better baseball player. He was a scholarship student and in the top 10 percent of his class, he had won honors in art and creative writing, and his greatest acclaim had been as a three-heat winner in the All-American Soap Box Derby.

Dawkins also had proved his toughness and determination long before he started playing competitive athletics when he was stricken with polio at age 11, causing a slight curvature to his spine and weakening his right side. Rather than allowing it to foreclose his athletic ambitions, he tirelessly engaged in a program of lifting barbells (there were none of the sophisticated weight rehabilitation programs that exist today) and conquered the effects of the disease, while also starting to enlarge his very slight frame. Still, a doctor told him to forget about football, but he refused to heed the advice and within a year was playing quarterback for his junior high school team.

At first, Dawkins did not want to go to West Point. He was pushed in its direction by Cranbrook's athletic director Fred Campbell, who also was his football and baseball coach. Campbell, a tough marine veteran of Iwo Jima during World War II, saw an inner toughness that belied Pete's slight build and budding athletic gifts. He insisted that a reluctant Dawkins accompany him on a visit to West Point prior to his senior year and then got only a lukewarm reception from Blaik when they showed up unannounced. They left a film of some of Dawkins' football achievements, passed a few nice words, and that was it. No promises, no encouragement.

Dawkins' attitude toward West Point changed in his senior year at Cranbrook after he began corresponding with Larry Asbury, a friend who had been a year ahead of him and who then was a plebe at the Military Academy. Asbury's descriptions about his life were very positive, even for a plebe whose existence by tradition at that time never was very comfortable. It wasn't long before the Academy had become Dawkins' first choice.

Advisers at West Point weren't that eager that he come at that time, suggesting that he spend a year in a prep school. He was just 17 at the time, the minimum age for admission, and it was felt he might be too young to compete. Dawkins wouldn't be put off and insisted on forging ahead to secure an appointment. Still, to cover himself, he secured admission to Michigan and Yale, his back-up schools.

Blaik still was skeptical that Dawkins could become an Army football player. He called Cranbrook's football program "silk stocking," meaning he didn't believe it could produce players who would succeed in the rugged level of competition at which West Point played. It didn't help that Dawkins was a gangly 17-year-old, still in the process of building his body from that of a 95-pound high school freshman with little visible muscle structure to that of a 170-pound athlete who still was growing physically.

Blaik, in his book *You Have to Pay the Price*, wrote of Dawkins' determination: "It was my lack of interest, Pete said later, that first made West Point a challenge to him, one he was unwilling to pass up."

Yet, the more Blaik researched Dawkins' background, the more impressed he became with Dawkins' character and tenacity. Finally, with time running out for admission, Blaik himself interceded with Dawkins' congressman and secured an appointment.

That was the easy part. As his plebe season unfolded in 1955, Blaik's negative assessment of Dawkins' football aptitude didn't change. He started most of the games for the plebe team at quarterback, but his passing skills were unimpressive, and he was even worse on defense. This didn't bode well for his football future at West Point because the substitution rules at that time forced players to play both offense and defense. When Blaik evaluated him after the season, he called him "hopeless."

"He isn't a good enough passer to make a varsity quarterback, and I never saw a worse defensive player," Blaik told his staff. "My inclination is to cut him."

One of his assistant coaches urged caution. "Let's see what we can do with him in spring practice," he said, and Blaik relented.

Dawkins languished as the fourth- or fifth-string quarterback in spring drills, and Blaik quietly told him he had little chance to succeed.

"I was shattered, literally," he said. "The center of my life was competitive sports, and football had become my favorite. In a conversation that lasted less than 30 seconds, my hopes for the future were dashed. It was like a blow to the solar plexus. To this day, I believe it was because I looked so crestfallen that Colonel Blaik allowed me to remain on the squad, but only by reporting in the fall as a scrum running back."

It wasn't until Dawkins returned some punts so well during a preseason scrimmage in 1956 that Blaik began reevaluating his talents.

"They kicked the ball to me and sent 11 guys to cover it, and I would get creamed," he said. "It happened again and again, with the same result. But I made a pact with myself that if my lot in life was not to be the starting quarterback, then I would become the best scrum running back on the punt return team. I put my heart and soul in it in the practices and learned how to avoid those tacklers. That was the break I needed, and all sorts of good things began to happen."

Blaik soon saw the skills of a natural runner, and he made Dawkins the fifth-string right halfback. He didn't play enough as a sophomore to earn a varsity letter. Still, he got a half dozen carries and turned half of those into touchdowns. One came at Michigan before his family and friends, though the Wolverines blew out the Cadets, 48–14.

Dawkins no longer wore the "hopeless" tag because he worked tirelessly in spring practice to improve himself. He became the starting right halfback when the 1957 season began. It was then, Blaik later recalled, that Dawkins began exhibiting his hallmark poise and confidence that brought such inspiring leadership to the 1958 team.

125

Still, that season he played second fiddle to Anderson, who was such a gifted runner that in his first varsity season, he broke Glenn Davis' single-season rushing record. Anderson had such a natural running style that it didn't even appear that he was moving fast. But when he was stopped, it was after he had gained an average of more than six yards per carry that season.

Dawkins, who had grown to 6'1" and 197 pounds, found his own niche in his role as Army's "triple-threat" back because he ran (665 yards for a 5.4 average and eight touchdowns), he utilized his left-handed passing skills (5 of 12 for 88 yards and a touchdown), he led the team in pass receptions (11 for 225 yards, three TDs), he was an unselfish blocker for Anderson, and he played solid defense. Dawkins and Anderson provided Army with one of the nation's most productive backfields in 1957 by scoring 25 touchdowns.

Even with that fine season, the almost instant notoriety Dawkins gained the following year was in stark contrast to his meager national standing when the preseason pundits were discussing Army's football chances in 1958. They talked first about Anderson, then about the Anderson-Dawkins pairing, but they never mentioned either when sizing up potential Heisman Trophy candidates. Even on his own team, Dawkins was still the "other" halfback to Anderson.

Of course, all of those discussions were carried on without the knowledge that Blaik had reworked his offense and had given his team a great tactical advantage with the Lonely End offense.

"Every team we played that year had to change its defense to play us," Dawkins said of the effect the new offense had on Army's opponents. "They all had one-game strategies, with a short time to prepare them. Their players wound up doing a lot of guessing on the run about their assignments, or they hesitated in carrying them out because they were unsure of what to do. That led to a lack of confidence and too many mistakes. Putting all of that together, we became an unheralded team on a sky-rocket ride.

"What Colonel Blaik really accomplished was the product of one of football's great minds, a coaching genius who long has been a member of the College Football Hall of Fame because he always found a way to win, whether he had sufficient resources."

In reality, Blaik opened the door for Dawkins' meteoric 1958 season. Spinning off that was Dawkins' ability to capitalize on the opportunity to produce as the team's principal running threat, to provide leadership as its captain, and to combine all of that with his tremendous facility to project himself in such a unique manner. Put together, it spelled Heisman Trophy.

Supplementing all of that was a spirit of unselfishness that was reflective of the team's great character. Anderson had to give way to Dawkins as the principle running back because Anderson was a superior blocker. Of course, Anderson also was a better runner, but Blaik reasoned that he would be more valuable blocking for Dawkins than Dawkins would be blocking for him. He was absolutely correct, but some of Anderson's great talent as a runner was sacrificed, and, as it turned out, it cost him an All-America selection. He had received some mention the previous year and was on the list of "potentials."

Anderson never complained, and that key piece of leadership was not lost on either the players or the coaches. At the time, they figured he would get his full shot in 1959 as a senior, but that never happened because a knee injury hobbled him for much of the season.

The last important piece of Blaik's 1958 Lonely End puzzle was Joe Caldwell, a six-foot, 156-pound quarterback. Some said he looked almost pitiful with his skinny arms and legs and his lack of size that made him appear more like the team's mascot than one of its key players. He soon earned the nickname "Urchin" because of his smallish build. But Blaik called him the best passer he ever coached. In the 1958 Lonely End season, he completed 54 of 120 passes for 1,097 yards and eight touchdowns.

It also helped that both Dawkins and Anderson were fine passers whenever the team used a halfback run-option play. It had always been a staple in Blaik's offense, and it is no coincidence that his greatest running backs also were deft passers. In 1958, Anderson utilized his constant threat as a running back to complete 10 of 15 for 141 yards and four touchdowns.

Blaik's initial worries about Caldwell's slim varsity experience were soon relieved, and Caldwell displayed a steady hand as a playcaller. Dawkins helped him immensely with his great ability throughout the season to diagnose defensive tendencies on the run and figure out what would work against them. It was an invaluable contribution that never received any notoriety. Without it, it is doubtful whether the team would have enjoyed its great success, and that would have slowed Dawkins' march to the Heisman Trophy.

"With all the pieces in place, on any given day when healthy, we could stand up to anyone," Dawkins said. "We had some very good players in Anderson, Carpenter, Caldwell, Don Usry, the other end, fullback Harry Walters, guard Bob Novogratz. Center Bill Rowe anchored a line that averaged 6'2" and 210 pounds, certainly not overwhelming in size, but smart and whipsaw tough."

Substitutes such as Russ Waters, the No. 2 Lonely End, and Steve Waldrop, who spelled Dawkins, also strengthened the team. Two other replacements were sophomore guards George Joulwon and Al Vanderbush. In two tours in South Vietnam, Joulwon was awarded two Silver Stars, three Bronze Stars (one with an Oak Leaf Cluster), the Commendation Medal, and 14 Air Medals. He finished his career as a four-star general and supreme Allied commander in Europe after commanding V Corps and the Southern Command during Operations Desert Shield and Desert Storm. Vanderbush was cocaptain of the 1960 team with Frank Gibson, and he later was a distinguished West Point athletic director during the nineties.

127

"We were not highly touted so we surprised some opponents early in the season," Dawkins said. "Later on, that wasn't the case, but we also had some luck because we had no depth, just 11 or 12 warriors. If someone got hurt, we were in trouble. Fortunately, we had no long-term serious injuries to our starters, and we were able to maintain our momentum throughout the season, not always easily. But we still had enough not to allow anyone to beat us."

The contributions of the entire Corps of Cadets—West Point's famed "12th man"—also played a huge role. While Dawkins' leadership and personality had its effect within Army's locker room and on the playing field, and he was lionized in the media, Anderson says the corps fueled so much of the emotion that sparked that 1958 team. "It was everywhere, it was a magical time," he recalled. "You couldn't get away from it. Walking from class or around the post, cadets would stop you and let you know how much they were behind the team. In front of the barracks, someone planted miniature tombstones with the names of our opponents. Their emotion was palpable, even to us on the field. We could feel their energy, and that kept us going.

"Pete supplied his own dynamic leadership, often by pulling off the right play at just the right time, and that just fueled our confidence. It swept through the team and helped to make us believe that we couldn't be beaten."

The Lonely End offense had shocked the media and the spectators who jammed Michie Stadium on a dank mid-September Saturday. In fact, a rainy morning had caused Blaik to reconsider unveiling his new offense until his team played on a dry field, but when the rain subsided, he went ahead with his plan.

And what a plan it was! South Carolina, an experienced team that had beaten Duke the previous week, had absolutely no idea how to cope with it. The Gamecocks spent much of the game debating how to cover the far-flanked Carpenter on his pass patterns, both as primary receiver and decoy. In the meantime, Caldwell and Anderson had a field day passing to Carpenter, Dawkins, and Usry.

Army rolled up 344 rushing yards and 185 by passing. In addition to his four touchdowns, Dawkins gained 113 rushing yards and an almost-instant wave of publicity that the new offense had generated.

While everyone still was trying to figure out how the offense worked, Army blanked Penn State 26–0 the following week. Dawkins scored two more touchdowns, one on a 53-yard pass from Caldwell, while the Lonely End offense again dazzled foe and spectator alike. Army scored all of its points in the first half, completing nine of eleven passes for 256 yards and rushing for another 93 yards.

The Lore of the Lonely End and Dawkins Fever hit a peak the following week when the Cadets defeated Notre Dame 14–2 at South Bend, only the second time that rivalry had ever been played on the Notre Dame campus. Army grabbed a 6–0 lead in the first quarter and gave up a safety early in the second half. Dawkins' touchdown with seven seconds to play, set up with his 23-yard pass reception, clinched the victory.

It was Blaik's custom on long trips to keep his team together at the hotel in the evening after the game. But he allowed his players, battered and bruised from the physical effects of the tough game against a more talented opponent, to have an evening on the town, with the only admonition, "Remember, we have another game next week."

128

"He had never done that before," Anderson recalled. "But it was the right thing at the right time for us after not only a tough game, but after we beat a team like Notre Dame. He allowed us to enjoy that victory on our own, and that had such a great effect on the team that I believed it carried over for the rest of the season."

Two weeks later, the Cadets suffered their only blemish that season in a 14–14 tie against Pitt. Dawkins had a deep thigh injury and participated in just one play—as a defensive back on the first half's final play, when he gave up a 57-yard touchdown pass that cut Army's lead to 14–7. Pitt tied the score in the second half. Afterward, Dawkins publicly berated himself for his error and took all the blame for his team's not winning the game. This was the other side of Dawkins' personality—the ferocious competitor who hated to lose or tie because of his own mental error.

"I wouldn't mind it so much if I missed a block or tackle," he said, "but I just goofed off mentally. I didn't cover [Pitt's John] Flara properly because I miscalculated the way they were lining up, and he got past me for the score."

Dawkins redeemed himself the following week with his most electric performance that year against Rice University in Houston, Texas. With less than a minute to play, he caught a 25-yard pass from Caldwell and outraced Rice's secondary for a game-winning, 61-yard touchdown play.

The score was tied 7–7 with just over a minute to play when Army blocked a Rice field goal and got the ball at its 24-yard line. With time left for three or four plays, the exhausted Cadets elected to try and quickly pass their way down the field. Caldwell's pass to Anderson gained 12 yards, and the next pass was incomplete. But Dawkins, as he had done all season, saw a flaw in the defense and suggested to Caldwell how he could take advantage of it.

Blaik, in his book *You Have to Pay the Price*, related what happened next:

"On the second pass play, Dawkins sensed from the way the Rice deep left man [safety] was playing him that he could feint him to the outside and veer back and get loose down the middle. In the huddle, he tipped Caldwell, and the play was called . . . Dawkins faked to the outside, reversed sharply to the inside, broke down the middle and took the ball at full speed on the Rice 35, one step beyond the Rice half-back. Then Pete raced for home like one of those old cavalry horses at Fort Bliss, stampeding across the desert toward a corral. On the 10-yard line, the pursuing [Don] Bucek tried to tackle Dawkins from behind. Bucek's arm reached for Pete's heels, found one of them, and almost tripped him. For one black instant Pete seemed about to fall. But he managed to keep his feet and get home free. . . ."

Army won 14–7 after Harry Walters kicked the extra point, and Dawkins said that game was the most memorable in a season filled with memorable games.

The following week, Dawkins cemented his Heisman Trophy with a stirring performance against Villanova. He broke a scoreless tie in the second quarter with an 80-yard punt return for a touchdown, he caught a 46-yard touchdown pass from Caldwell, and he later caught a 48-yard pass to set up his 6-yard scoring run in a 26–0 victory.

The Army-Navy game was the season's finale, and it was played on a clear, bitterly cold day before 102,000 at Philadelphia's Municipal Stadium and a huge national television audience, which also got to see what all the oohing and aahing were about with the Lonely End and Dawkins.

129

Downtown Athletic Club

Dawkins at the Heisman Award Ceremony. Behind the Podium is Master of Ceremonies Al Helfer. Dawkins cemented his Heisman Trophy with his performance against Villanova.

The game started as a disaster for Army and Dawkins. While returning the opening kickoff, he collided with a blocker when it appeared he was about to burst into an open field and run unmolested to Navy's end zone. The ball popped loose, and Navy recovered on the Cadets' 40-yard line.

The Mids had a future Heisman Trophy winner of their own, running back Joe Bellino, and he led them to a touchdown and a 6–0 lead. Twice more in the first quarter, Army lost the ball on turnovers, and visions of past upsets by Navy under such circumstances suddenly flashed through Blaik's mind like a wide-awake bad dream. He certainly had never forgotten the near miss that three-touchdown underdog Navy almost pulled off in 1946 when it came within five yards and a few seconds of defeating the Blanchard and Davis team in its final game.

But the 1958 Lonely End team was a poised unit, and it never panicked while shutting down the Mids without any further scoring. However, Anderson, not Dawkins, became the key offensive performer, pounding the Navy defense for 89 yards in 29 carries. He ended two long drives with touchdowns.

Dawkins, meanwhile, was a total contributor with his own blocking, and he got more of the running load as the game went to its late stages and the tired Navy defense retreated under the pounding of a relatively fresh pair of legs. Carpenter also was used more as a decoy, and Caldwell passed mostly to Dawkins and Usry. Usry got Army's clinching touchdown in the final two minutes when he intercepted a pass by Navy quarterback Joe Tranchini and returned it for a touchdown.

Dawkins, with a bit of dramatic flair, put the finishing touch on his astounding season by passing for the two-point conversion to Anderson for a 22–6 victory. Army nailed down the Lambert Trophy as the East's best team as well as the No. 3 national ranking. Dawkins, along with Anderson and Novogratz, who later won the Bronze Star during a combat tour in Vietnam, was selected to the All-America team.

After the game, MacArthur, who watched on television in his suite at the Waldorf Towers Hotel in New York City, wired Blaik and the Army team:

"In the long history of West Point athletics, there has never been a greater triumph. It has brought pride and happiness and admiration to millions of Army rooters throughout the world. Tell Captain Dawkins and his indomitable team they have written their names in golden letters on the tablets of football fame. For you, my dear old friend, it marks one of the most glorious moments of your peerless career. There is no substitute for victory."

A week after the Army-Navy game, Dawkins was named the winner of the 1958 Heisman Trophy. He again dazzled everyone with his poise and ability to articulate his feelings about all that he had accomplished and how much it involved his school, his teammates, and his coaches. He was riveting for those who had not heard him and compelled the same rapt attention from those who had.

It had all seemed so neat and easy to those who marveled at Dawkins' achievements that season, but he had a penchant for making things look that way. For example, until his Heisman year, few knew that he played hockey. He had never

Showing his all-around versatili-
ty as an athlete, Dawkins also
starred in hockey at West Point
and played rugby and cricket as
a Rhodes Scholar at Oxford.

played the sport until he came to West Point, and then he won three varsity letters. In his senior year, he was an all-East defenseman, and as a junior and senior, he was the East's highest-scoring defenseman. In his career, he scored 95 points on 40 goals and 55 assists.

After graduating from West Point in 1959, he went to Oxford for three years on a Rhodes Scholarship. His advisers worried that his fame as a football player would work against his getting a scholarship because, as he said later, the committee was comprised of "cobwebish intellectuals."

"I had brushed up on my Plato and Keats, and on the American economic system—questions I was sure they'd ask me," he recalled. "The first question was, 'How did the Lonely End in Army's unique offensive formations get his signals?' I thought my chances were down when I declined to tell them, but I managed to make the grade."

Dawkins earned two degrees at Oxford. But he created his biggest stir three months after he arrived in England when he shook up the staid British rugby establishment by becoming so adept at their game that he was picked to play for Oxford against archrival Cambridge in England's version of the Army-Navy game. Oxford won, 9–3.

The British were particularly agog with his "line-outs," the manner in which the ball is put into play. English rugby players could accurately throw the ball five or ten yards, but he threw it like an American football—long, arching passes similar to those he had thrown at Cranbrook and West Point that sailed into the hands of waiting teammates far downfield. This innovation, still widely used in English rugby today, was hailed by British sportswriters as the "Yank's torpedo pass." But it was not only his skill but also his willingness to become a part of the game that made Dawkins so popular.

While Dawkins was wowing the English with his rugby skills, American military involvement had begun to escalate in Vietnam. Early American commitments were mainly in the form of military "advisers" attached to units of South Vietnam's army to help them plan and then actively run their military operations in the field.

The army had not been involved in combat for 10 years—since the end of the Korean War. It was different this time because the conflict was basically a guerilla war. No large units were involved—that would come in the late sixties when there was a full-scale escalation—so the army sent many of its brightest young officers, many of them recent graduates of West Point, to handle the advisory work and gain combat experience.

After Dawkins returned from Oxford in 1962, he immersed himself in building his military career, including becoming an honors graduate at the army's ranger school in 1963. He served as a company commander and assistant operations officer in the 82nd Airborne Division before attending the army's language school to learn Vietnamese. Upon graduation, he was dispatched to South Vietnam as part of the Military Assistance Command, Vietnam, in 1965. It is said that he surveyed the war zone and told a reporter, "This is the big stadium. This is the varsity. I want to be in on it."

As previously noted, he was assigned to the First Airborne Battalion of South Vietnam's army, its most decorated unit. Its military heritage extended back to the Indochina War of liberation against the French, following the end of World War II. Most of the unit's noncommissioned officers were Cambodians; most of its officers were from North Vietnam. Dawkins described its mission as that akin to a "fire brigade." It was the nation's strategic reserve force, and wherever there was a major battle, it would be dispatched by helicopters from its camp in Saigon. "It was," he declared, "the best fighting unit in South Vietnam's army, and it fought in all four corners of South Vietnam, from the Cambodian border to the central coast of the South China Sea."

Dawkins was a captain in both the U.S. Army and the South Vietnam army, and he wore the captain bars and airborne insignia of both. He totally acclimated himself to those he was trying to assist, eating their food and sleeping in a hammock next to Major Dong, the battalion's South Vietnamese commander. He also made several jumps in combat with the unit as it tangled in hard fighting with both hard-core Vietcong and North Vietnam's army.

Dawkins' role as an adviser to the unit, like the roles of all U.S. advisers, was two-pronged—an official role, and what he actually did. "The official role was to provide counsel and advice on unit training," he said. "In combat situations, we were to be collaborators with the commanding officer on tactical decisions and to control the fire support from artillery, close air, and naval gunfire. We also directed the choppers bringing in men and supplies."

Boundaries of responsibility sometimes got very fuzzy during battle, such as the aforementioned action involving the First Battalion and the U.S. Marines against a North Vietnamese regiment, where Dawkins took control of the entire operation. That was the second prong of responsibility—doing what was necessary to succeed in battle, the primary mission of any action, regardless of the chain of command.

The first, and sometimes the biggest, problems the advisers had to confront were the differences in culture and military orthodoxy. The training element of their mission was supposed to alleviate the latter; the former never was solved. Dawkins related the story of how the South Vietnam army chefs prepared chickens for cooking—they stretched a chicken like a rubber band and then systematically chopped it into pieces from top to bottom. Everything was thrown into the pot for cooking, including the head and even the toenails from the chicken's feet. It required some deft manipulation to extract the inedible pieces at mealtime.

"I thought I could teach them our way of preparing chicken, so I gathered them around me. I cut away the various edible parts of the chicken just as an American butcher would do and threw away the feet, the head, and the other parts of no value to us," he related. "They sat and watched so intently that I really believed I had gotten the idea across to them.

"When we finished, I said, 'OK, you do it.' And they went right back to stretching the chicken and chopping it up in pieces like they did before I tried to change their way."

Forgetting cultural differences, Dawkins had high regard for the Vietnamese troops with whom he worked.

"The Vietnamese troops we worked with were as good a group of fighting men as there were anywhere," he said. "They were enormously courageous . . . you could see them carrying .57-millimeter recoilless weapons that weighed almost as much as they did along with a can of ammunition and a pack strapped to their back while they double-timed through the jungle. They asked very little and performed very well for us when I was there."

There was a commonality—the South Vietnamese soldiers and their officers and their American advisers shared the perils of battle. Time and again, Dawkins saw the South Vietnamese soldiers perform over and above their capacity, to the point that their actions could easily be termed "heroic" or "valorous."

Was he ever scared during a battle?

"Certainly," he replied. "Everyone is. But it is a controlled fear. Fear is the counterpoint of my training. They play off each other. The most powerful emotion to me was: what was my responsibility to my soldiers? It's always been that way. If one person was involved, chances are he'd be run over by fear. But understanding that other people's lives are in your trust, then dealing with that is what the military and West Point is all about. That's a real reservoir of strength. You fall back on feeling that you are not going to let down those soldiers, and that's often when you surprise yourself with what you can do.

"Men in battle often perform in ways neither they nor you would ever expect," Dawkins said. "One of the great lessons I learned on the battlefield was that you never could predict the one who would have the courage to do the decisive thing. More often than not, it was the person who you don't expect who will step forward and perform above and beyond the call of duty."

The major reason, Dawkins believes, is not because of a cause or principles but a sense that something needs to be done and they say to themselves, "If not me, then who?" Another factor is the personal loyalty they have to each other, that they are not going to let down or disappoint their buddies.

Who are the people who do these deeds? We saw them by the score during the terrorist attacks on New York's World Trade Center and the Pentagon on September 11, 2001—firefighters, police officers, and emergency service people willing to walk into doomed buildings to try and bring out survivors—and, sadly, many perished with those whom they tried to save.

"One of my classmates, Humbert 'Rocky' Versace, is the best example," Dawkins said. "He was awarded a posthumous Medal of Honor in 2002 for some of the most incredible deeds you could imagine. He was an argumentative, hardheaded guy at West Point. He had made captain and had decided to leave the army and become a priest after his tour in Vietnam ended.

135

"But a week before he was scheduled to leave, he was captured by the Vietcong after a bitter battle. He was severely wounded, but the Vietcong never dressed his wounds. Instead, they dragged him and other prisoners around the country for a year and a half, torturing them and forcing them to live in horrid conditions.

"Rocky refused to buckle under to their demands that he sign a statement refuting his country and what it stood for. He was fluent in Vietnamese so he talked and debated with them all the time, and the logic and intensity of his arguments just infuriated them. Finally, they put him in a bamboo cage that was just the same size as he was, meaning he could not move. They starved him and finally decided to execute him. The night before it happened, he was separated from his fellow prisoners and thrown into the jungle, where the darkness is unlike any you have ever experienced. If his captors expected him to plead for mercy to be with his fellow prisoners on the final night of his life, they were bitterly disappointed because from that dark jungle came the song "God Bless America." The next day, the Vietcong executed him.

"Would any of us who knew him as a cadet ever guess that he was capable of such courage and valor? Probably not, because there are no absolute models. But if there were, then the standout is Bill Carpenter, who called in a napalm attack on his own position to help save his troops."

In one of the ironies of war, Dawkins had originally been scheduled for assignment as an adviser to the unit that Carpenter ultimately was assigned to. But Dawkins was pulled off the list to work as part of a team that had started what became the Pacification Program in South Vietnam, and he was replaced by his former teammate. "When I didn't come, then Hank Emerson, commander of the 502nd Infantry, gave the job to Bill," he said.

Of course, Emerson was a story by himself. A West Point classmate of Blanchard and Davis, he had distinguished himself during the early months of the Korean War as a member of the Fifth Regimental Combat Team by winning a Silver Star, two Bronze Stars, a Purple Heart, and a Commendation Ribbon. Dawkins worked for him with the 82nd Airborne Division at Fort Campbell, Kentucky, before both received Vietnam assignments. During his battle tour in Vietnam, where he encountered Carpenter, he was awarded three more Silver Stars, three Bronze Stars, a Legion of Merit, and four Air Medals. Emerson retired from the army as a lieutenant general in 1977 after commanding the XVIII Airborne Corps.

Carpenter, the famed Lonely End, became one of the most courageous soldiers in the history of the U.S. Army. As a cadet, he had the facial profile of movie actor Tab Hunter, one of Hollywood's heartthrobs of that time. The Lonely Hearts Club—long before the dating services began—made him its No. 1 pinup. All of that flustered him no end, as did the kidding from his teammates, who nicknamed him "Lonesome George" because of his unique position on the football field.

Carpenter's military career is a stirring story of the meaning of Duty, Honor, and Country. His willingness to forego opportunities to accumulate advanced degrees from civilian universities or accept top-level staff jobs in the Pentagon because he preferred duty with the troops set him apart from many career officers,

Captain William S. Carpenter shakes hands with President Lyndon Johnson after being recommended for the Congressional Medal of Honor. Carpenter bravely called a napalm strike on his own company's position in an effort to fight off Vietcong forces. Also pictured is General William C. Westmoreland, commander of U.S. forces in Vietnam at that time.

including Dawkins. It even included his refusal to play service football after playing for an army post team in 1962.

When the army cut orders for him to do it again in 1963, he threatened to resign and sign with the NFL's Baltimore Colts, who had drafted him after his college career ended. "If I am going to be forced to play football, I'm going to do it for a lot more than $200 a month," he said of the approximate net pay that first lieutenants received at that time.

The alternative was duty as an adviser in South Vietnam, and he took it, the first of two combat tours in that country during which he was awarded every combat medal given by the army except the Medal of Honor. He was nominated for that, too, during his second tour but let it be known that he didn't believe that he had earned it. In its stead, he was awarded the Distinguished Service Cross, the nation's second-highest combat medal.

During his first tour, in 1963–1964, he was wounded twice, once by a piece of shrapnel, the other time when he was shot in the right arm. He said later that after he was shot, he used his nonthrowing, or left, arm to toss a couple of grenades at the enemy soldier, and emptied a clip of carbine ammunition and the magazine from his .45 pistol into the foxhole where the soldier had hidden. He returned home with a Silver Star, a Bronze Star, a Commendation Medal, an Air Medal, two Purple Hearts, and the Combat Infantryman's Badge.

He served again in Vietnam in 1966–1967, and during that tour, nothing set him apart more than a decision he made on June 9, 1966, to call down an air attack on his own position to save his troops. As a captain at the time, he commanded Charley Company, Second Battalion, 502nd Airborne Infantry Regiment of the 101st Airborne Division near Toumorong in South Vietnam's Central Highlands. His troops surprised what they believed were stragglers from a North Vietnam regiment and began inflicting severe casualties for the first half hour of the battle. As the fight progressed, though, his men started to be outgunned by heavy-caliber machine guns and mortars, none of which they had at their disposal. It was then that he realized that his company was in the midst of the enemy regiment, not at its tail, and that it was badly outnumbered and surrounded.

His unit had taken casualties, and trying to leave a battlefield with dead and wounded was not feasible. Nor would he leave behind the wounded to be captured or killed by a vicious enemy. Needing help to relieve the enemy's pressure that began to shrink his perimeter and infiltrate his positions, he called for air support and was told by the aircraft spotter that there were two planes available to assist him.

"Watch for my yellow smoke marker," he told the spotter, setting the means to mark the target that was in the midst of his own troops. Within seconds after he tossed the smoke grenade, an air force jet, carrying two canisters of napalm under its wings, came swooping across the treetops toward the smoke. Carpenter had no way of knowing the support he was getting would be in the form of napalm, and the pilot didn't know that the smoke marker was right in the midst of Carpenter's position.

When a canister tumbled end over end like a poor punt and hit the ground, the jungle exploded in sheets of flame. What enemy survivors remained scattered in all directions, and their attack on Carpenter's position ceased, allowing him and his unit to tighten their positions and survive until they were rescued later that night. Miraculously, none of his men were touched by the napalm. His company suffered just eight losses and a number of wounded among its 100 men, but the unit survived intact.

Asked later by reporters why he did such a thing, Carpenter bristled that the answer to this question wasn't self-evident. "Because it was available, because the enemy was overrunning us, and because retreating and leaving our wounded behind was out of the question," he replied.

Nor was that the final time he distinguished himself in Vietnam with his heroism. In 1967, a transport plane in which he was riding made a belly landing at Saigon's Tan Son Nhut Airport, and an army major aboard suffered a broken ankle in the crash. Carpenter carried him from the wrecked plane on his shoulders.

Along with the Distinguished Service Cross that he received during that tour of duty, he left Vietnam with another Silver Star, three Air Medals for missions flown in helicopters, the Joint Service Commendation Medal, and the Legion of Merit Award.

Carpenter's story also dovetails closely with that of Don Holleder, another All-American end who had preceded him at West Point. He was an All-American in 1954 as a junior and looked forward to repeating in 1955 until Blaik told him before spring drills that he would become the team's quarterback.

"Colonel," he said, "I have never played in the backfield in my life."

Blaik knew that, but he had already weighed all of Holleder's assets: he was the team's best athlete who could adequately make the switch in positions; he was also its best leader, the key in his book to playing the position; and he was smart enough to run the offense.

"I knew that Holly was the only player we had who could provide us with the bright, aggressive, inspirational leadership at the key position on the team," he said later. "I also knew that if he stayed at end, his marvelous skills as a receiver would be wasted because we had no one to throw him the ball."

Blaik also had one other motive. He wanted someone to match Navy's brilliant quarterback, George Welsh, so his team would have a fighting chance to beat the Mids, always Army's most important opponent. The previous fall, Welsh led Navy's famed Team Named Desire to a stirring 28–20 victory over one of Blaik's best teams of the fifties, and he seemed poised to do it again in 1955.

Blaik left the final decision to Holleder, with the proviso that if he were unhappy with the experiment, he could return to his end position. Holleder, in a supreme act of courage, agreed and forfeited his opportunity for a second All-America selection. His lack of work and experience, particularly in the passing game, showed throughout the season, and he often faced heavy criticism for the

139

Don Holleder.

USMA Library Special Collections and Archives Division

inconsistent way he ran Army's offense, some of it coming from within the usually loyal Corps of Cadets.

He won his first two starts. Then, what had been termed the "Great Experiment" just as quickly was called "Blaik's Folly," after a 26–2 loss to a poor

Michigan team. A couple of days after the game, Holleder went to Blaik's office with tears in his eyes and told his coach he feared all the stories questioning his ability were right.

"I thought you played well," Blaik told him, and that might have given him enough courage to survive even when he didn't complete a pass the following week in a 13–0 loss to Syracuse. But the season turned around and became a ringing success, capped by a 14–6 upset victory over Navy that cost the Mids an Orange Bowl bid.

There were no All-America honors, but Holleder won the Swede Nelson Award given to college football's "most unselfish and courageous player."

Twelve years later in Vietnam, Major Don Holleder, while flying in a helicopter, saw wounded American soldiers trying to reach safety. He ordered the chopper to land and led his troops down a streambed, hoping to reach the wounded men before they were attacked by the enemy. As they were advancing, Holleder and his men were raked by automatic weapons fire, and he was badly wounded. Still, he commanded the successful rescue mission, but he died the next day from his wounds.

He is buried in Arlington National Cemetery, and the Holleder Center at West Point currently houses the Academy's basketball and hockey arenas. Interestingly, Carpenter, Holleder, and Dawkins are enshrined in the College Football Hall of Fame; and Dawkins became the first recipient of the Major Donald

141

Linz Photographers

Pete Dawkins shares a light moment at the White House with President Ronald Reagan. Dawkins had just announced himself as a candidate for the office of U.S. Senator from New Jersey.

General Dawkins with his wife, Judith, answering questions at a press conference after his retirement review.

Holleder Award, given by the Rochester (New York) Press-Radio Club to a person "whose active life has exhibited the highest level of sportsmanship, character, courage, and achievement consistent with the name and ideals of Major Holleder."

Dawkins left Vietnam in 1966 a much-decorated officer with the Legion of Merit (with Oak Leaf Cluster), two Bronze Stars (with Oak Leaf Clusters), an Air Medal, the Joint Service Commendation Medal, the Army Commendation Medal, and the Vietnamese Cross of Gallantry (with two Gold Palms and one Gold Star).

Several years after his Vietnam experience, Dawkins was asked how his football experience carried over into his military career, particularly serving in combat situations.

"It's things like knowing that you have to pay the price and master fundamentals," he said. "That you have to sacrifice, that it's a matter of determination and attitude, that teamwork is indispensable. They are part and parcel of what you learn on the playing fields of West Point, the things that are the difference between victory on the battlefield, and defeat."

Dawkins' subsequent military career was a variety of troop, staff, and educational assignments, and in 1981, he became the army's youngest brigadier general when he was appointed deputy director of the army's Strategy, Plans, and Policy Directorate. Two years later, he stunned many who still believed he someday would be chief of staff by retiring to pursue a high-profile business career, and he later made an unsuccessful run for the U.S. Senate in New Jersey.

Dawkins will always be remembered for his many achievements, including his Heisman Trophy and his heroism in battle. But his life was best summed up in the 1959 *Howitzer*, West Point's yearbook, where, beneath his picture, was written: "We have stood in awe of this man. But a triumph more enduring promoted him to this singular position: specifically, Pete firmly gripped our hands in deep and understanding friendship. Consequently, never was a task given to him not successfully accomplished; for as he cared, so also did we. We were not completely sagacious but we knew a great leader, a great friend, a great man."

143

Chapter 4
Roger Staubach

There has never been a college quarterback who enthralled an entire nation as Navy's Roger Staubach did during the 1963 season.

In fact, for most of the 1962 and 1963 seasons the feats that he performed on the football field exuded a magical quality that transposed the impossible to a form of football theater whose scripts challenged the best that any fiction writers could produce.

There was one big difference, though: what he did wasn't fiction. It just seemed that way because of his uncanny knack for producing successful, almost miracle finishes. He always seemed to perform the impossible before huge national audiences or in games of great significance. Such feats passed the true test for measuring greatness.

He earned the nickname Roger the "Dodger" by escaping football ambushes with his extraordinary physical skills and a determination to succeed. This drove defensive opponents into nearly apoplectic states of frenzy and frustration. No 60-minute football clock ever seemed capable of foiling his ability to produce victories where victories had no right to be produced.

But it wasn't all some unexplained magic that propelled his success. He was a great player, and great players perform great deeds. He did that during an unbelievable 1963 season to become only the fourth junior ever to win the Heisman Trophy, as well as a sack full of other awards.

Nearly 40 years after he played his last game at the Naval Academy, those who played with him or coached him still marvel at what he achieved that season. Others who could only watch him play are still equally awestruck about all they saw. Just to prove it wasn't all a fantasy, after four years of active duty service as a naval officer, including a tour in Vietnam's war zone, he reprised his collegiate feats a decade later as quarterback of the great Dallas Cowboys teams of the seventies. Tens of millions more became believers. In each instance his feats led him into the Halls of Fame that permanently honor the greatest players in both collegiate and professional football.

Becoming a Hall of Famer at any level requires tremendous skill and achievement, but it also must be seasoned with touches of good luck. That's what happened to Staubach; there were three instances early in his career where playing quarterback almost didn't happen. Had any of those occurred, there may well not have been a Staubach legend, at least not as we know it. As a freshman in high school, he wanted to be a running back or tight end and had never thought about playing quarterback. But his coach, Jim McCarthy, fortunately saw a talent and a penchant for leadership that Staubach wasn't aware he possessed and moved him to the position. Later it was a slipup over the results of a failed test for color blindness by a navy

**Midshipman
Roger Staubach.**

U.S. Naval Academy Archives

medical technician that allowed him to almost "sneak" into the Naval Academy. He was color-blind, and that should have disqualified him for admission to a school where he ultimately won the Heisman Trophy and became its greatest quarterback ever. But that almost didn't happen because his varsity coach, Wayne Hardin, watched him perform as a plebe, or freshman, quarterback and so admired his ability to run that he wanted to make him a running back. Only a strong dissent by former Navy running back Joe Bellino, one of the freshman coaches and winner of the 1960 Heisman Trophy, helped to change Hardin's mind.

Staubach's great career at Navy paved the way for his decade-long tenure with the Dallas Cowboys, which culminated in his being enshrined in pro football's Hall of Fame in Canton, Ohio.

His career as a quarterback didn't start to blossom until his senior year at Purcell High School in Cincinnati. "That changed my life, without a doubt," he said. "It happened again after my plebe season at the Naval Academy when coach Wayne Hardin wanted to put me on defense, and his coaching staff, principally Joe Bellino and George Welsh, argued forcibly for me to stay at quarterback. Their thinking prevailed, but I've always wondered what would have happened if coach Hardin had insisted that I play defense."

Staubach won his first start in high school, lost his second, and was moved to defense. He then broke his hand and didn't play again until the season's final game. Under McCarthy's system at that time, juniors played defense and seniors played offense, so in his junior year Roger was a defensive back and backup quarterback. He got the starting job in his senior year because his coaches admired both his athletic and leadership qualities.

But Roger quickly added a new dimension to Purcell's offense, which didn't have one running play for the quarterback—not even a quarterback sneak—by reverting to what he really wanted to do most: run with the ball after he dropped back to pass and didn't see an open receiver. He gained more than 500 rushing yards that season and earned his nickname, which followed him throughout his college and pro careers. The last 62 rushing yards were for the winning touchdown that earned Purcell the 1959 Cincinnati city championship.

He was pursued by several Big Ten schools, particularly Purdue, Ohio State, and Michigan, and by the two Cincinnati area colleges, Xavier and the University of Cincinnati. No coach tried harder and with more passion to recruit him than Woody Hayes at Ohio State. But Roger became wary of the huge Big Ten universities and the possibility of getting sidetracked from his twin aims of excelling in academics *and* athletics. In the end he agreed to accept an offer from Purdue because he believed that assistant coach Bobby DeMoss, who coached the quarterbacks, could make him a better player.

Through all of this, Navy assistant coach Rick Forzano also kept after him. He had gone to Purcell during Staubach's junior year to look at films of a center, Jerry Lawford, who now runs a branch office of Staubach's real estate firm in Texas. But Roger's play jumped out at him. He watched Roger excel at baseball later that day and was tremendously impressed with him as a person when he chatted with him.

When Forzano returned to Purcell the following year to review films of Staubach's games, he was determined to land him, though he still believed that Roger would go to Notre Dame because it was the only school he seemed to care about. But the Irish coaches showed no interest, and after a visit to the school, neither did Staubach. Later, they changed their minds, but it was too late because he had agreed to attend New Mexico Military Institute (NMMI) for a year's junior college preparation for the Naval Academy.

Forzano stayed on pins and needles. A low grade, by Naval Academy standards, on the English part of his college entrance examinations meant he'd have to prep for a year, and he didn't want to do that.

That made it tougher for Forzano. He later related: "I kept hoping we could change Roger's mind about not wishing to wait a year to enter the Naval Academy. Then one day he called and said that Purdue was his choice.

"I never thought he was serious about Purdue. I grabbed a plane to Cincinnati for one more talk with Roger. He still had doubts about the four-year service commitment that followed graduation . . . and he was dead set against a year at prep school.

"So out of the blue, I said, 'Roger, how about going to New Mexico Military Institute? It's a junior college and a fine school academically. You can go there on a football scholarship with no obligation to the Naval Academy. If you decide after a year you want to attend another school, you can transfer all of your credits and start as a sophomore.'"

Staubach had no great desire to attend the Naval Academy or even to serve in the navy until after he had visited Annapolis. Then he became more impressed with the atmosphere there than what he had seen at the Big Ten schools, primarily because of the great emphasis placed on academics. Like many boys his age, his study habits were not the best, and he believed that the Academy would sharpen those skills and allow him to succeed academically.

He was one of 20 Naval Academy prospects who attended NMMI that year. "I could have gotten into any school because in my college boards I had good scores, high math, medium English," Staubach said. "But they separated the scores and had us go to prep school. But I really think they wanted me to develop as an athlete, and prep school was the route."

When Staubach finally committed himself to NMMI and the Naval Academy, Forzano sent him a telegram: "Someday you are going to win the Heisman Trophy at Navy and have a battleship named after you."

Staubach responded by being named a junior college All-American quarterback that season, thanks in no small measure to the coaching of Bob Shaw. A great end in the National Football League in the forties and early fifties, Shaw harnessed Staubach's quarterback talents. "I was more of a running quarterback, a sort of maverick at the position because I ran so much," Staubach said. "We only threw the ball eight or ten times a game at Purcell, but Bob Shaw had a wide-open offense. He integrated my running ability with a sophisticated passing offense and enabled me to have a great season. It gave me enough confidence so that I had a head start on the other plebe quarterbacks when I got to Annapolis.

"But NMMI, a military school, gave me a great introduction to military life, and it taught me how to balance school, athletics, and my other activities. That's a big advantage going to the Naval Academy."

Staubach was finally talked into attending the Naval Academy by assistant coach Rick Forzano, partly because he was convinced the strict academic standards would improve his study habits.

U.S. Naval Academy Archives

While it wasn't until the fourth game of his sophomore season in 1962 that Staubach began to shine, those at the Naval Academy had known for more than a year that he was an exceptional player. His credentials as a junior college All-American had preceded him to Annapolis, and he methodically worked his way past 24 plebe quarterback prospects to become the starter. The plebe team won all but one game—the last, in the final seconds, to the University of Maryland.

His plebe coach was Dick Duden, a Hall of Fame end on Navy's great wartime teams of the mid-forties. He was a tough New Yorker who was like a drill sergeant in squaring away the plebes on what it took to be a Navy football player. He was assisted in that year by Bellino and Hal Spooner, both on six-month assignment as assistant coaches.

Spooner had been a very skilled technician at quarterback, and he, and later Doug Scovil on the varsity, helped to polish Staubach's game without taming his Roger the Dodger style of scrambling about to find a receiver or run for a big gain. That style captivated everyone who watched him in scrimmages against the varsity or in his plebe team games, and his legend began to grow.

He was often more than the varsity could handle with his unique playing style. No one at Navy had ever seen anything like it, including the varsity coach, Wayne Hardin. After Roger had made an astounding play, Hardin found himself thinking: "You are awful lucky to get away with that." A couple of years later, Hardin revamped his thinking. "I was lucky to have someone that great play for me."

There were times when scrimmages got pretty rough and Staubach became a target for the varsity's frustrations. One day he was continually embarrassing the varsity with his running and passing, and every time he crossed the goal line, the varsity players pounded him. Watching all of this was Rear Admiral John Davidson, the Naval Academy's superintendent. Finally, he couldn't stand seeing Staubach getting pummeled any longer. He walked right to the middle of the field, confronted a stunned Hardin, and barked: "Hey, Duden needs this kid for Saturday. Call off your dogs."

And he did.

None of this bothered Staubach. He always loved competition and never backed off when it got rough.

Nor was there any mistaking his desire to excel. Steve Belichick, a longtime assistant coach at Navy, recalled Staubach trying to get into the equipment room to get a football. It was near the end of his plebe year, and he had just finished spring drills with the varsity.

"What do you need a football for?" Belichick asked him.

"I want to throw," he replied.

"What for?" Belichick persisted. "It's a beautiful spring afternoon, spring football is over, there's a doubleheader on the baseball field. Why don't you go up there and relax?"

Staubach was having none of it, and he finally persuaded Belichick to go home and get him a football. They agreed to meet early in the afternoon in front of massive Dahlgren Hall. When Belichick arrived, Staubach, covered with sweat, came running toward him.

"I couldn't remember if you said the front or back of Dahlgren so I've been running between the two," Roger told him.

After Staubach's plebe season, Hardin and the varsity coaches wanted to make him a running back. Bellino said later that he offered such a vigorous dissent that Hardin relented and agreed to keep him at quarterback, though the position was very crowded.

"My point to the coaches was that Roger was an excellent runner; he had a good release of the ball, though not always in a tight spiral. But it always got to the receiver where it was supposed to be," Bellino recalled. "But most of all, he was a winner, and you can't teach an attribute that is probably the most important for any quarterback."

As his varsity career unfolded, his ability to consistently succeed was the key to Staubach's success. But he also had great natural talent for the position, to which he added his ability to get out in the open field and make good things happen. He ran with long, powerful strides and utilized a quick change of pace that accentuated deceptive speed. He never had blinding speed, but as his coaches said, "he was fast enough." He seemed ungainly as a runner at times, but his success sprung from an uncanny ability to switch direction and running pace after defenders had committed themselves to stopping him and could not recover their balance.

151

"He didn't look like he was going fast," said Tom Lynch, captain, center, and linebacker on the 1963 team, "but he disappointed a lot of would-be tacklers who thought they had him."

As a passer, he threw accurately from the pocket, on the run, or even when backing up, and he had great instincts that allowed him to use his speed and elusiveness to get free and find an open receiver when he was trapped. He would take off and become Roger the Dodger. All of this helped him to control a game by keeping defenses off balance and exercising last-second options that were keyed to his mobility.

Staubach's first experience playing with the varsity in spring drills of his plebe year was far from satisfying. He was fifth or sixth on the quarterback depth chart, and the coaches even tried him as a defensive back. Once again, the fates intervened because a shoulder injury suffered in a boxing class before his plebe year had recurred and so hampered him that he couldn't tackle nor raise his arm to defend against passes, and he returned to the quarterback derby.

Hardin was trying to figure out a way to either channel his ability into becoming a drop-back passer, as the coach favored, or to gin up the offense and make room for his great running ability. Sometime in the future, Hardin knew, Staubach would be his starting quarterback, but there seemed no great hurry to solve the problem. Incumbent starter Ron Klemick had led the Mids to a 7–3 record in 1961, and he fit Hardin's drop-back style.

Staubach won the quarter-
back job in his sophomore
year when he led the Mids
to victory by directing six
touchdown drives in a game
against Cornell.

But injuries to quarterbacks ahead of Staubach thinned the ranks, and when the team ended its 1962 preseason drills at Quonset Point Naval Air Base in Rhode Island, he was the No. 3 quarterback. That's where he stood in the season's fourth game against Cornell, having played only six minutes while Navy won just one of its first three games. His statistics were uninspiring: no completions in six attempts and minus 14 yards rushing. Hardin was desperate to get the team on a winning track, but that didn't happen until Klemick was injured in the first quarter against Cornell and Staubach replaced him.

What ensued was a preview of coming attractions for most of the rest of that season and for his wondrous 1963 Heisman Trophy year. Staubach directed six touchdown drives; completed nine of eleven passes for 99 yards and two touchdowns; scored another touchdown; and ran eight times for 89 yards, including the first of what would become his signature play for the rest of his career—an eye-popping gallop of 68 yards through most of Cornell's defense.

Later that season, during a trip to the West Coast to play Southern California, Admiral Davidson pointedly asked Hardin why, in light of Staubach's outstanding plebe season, he waited so long to give him some playing time.

"Experience," Hardin replied. "I always believe in going with experience, and he didn't have any. Luckily, the regular quarterback got hurt, and I had to put him in."

153

Staubach built on that "luck" the week after his debut against Cornell. He started against Boston College but was a bit shaky early in the game and Hardin replaced him with Klemick. "I think Wayne was trying to figure out what to do with a couple of senior quarterbacks, Klemick and Bruce Abel, sitting on the bench while a sophomore was doing all the playing," Staubach said. "When things didn't change while Ron was playing, he put me back in, and we won the game, 26–6. I had a couple of touchdown passes, but it was that game that convinced Wayne that I was for real."

He certainly was. Staubach's play and his natural leadership lit a fire under that Navy team, and it began playing with a vigor that surprised everyone. "He grew into the job," said Lynch. "It wasn't like he was a savior. He got his shot, he performed, and he grew into the role. Then, he started to do it week after week. That's when we started to really believe in his leadership and performance ability."

After Navy got a third straight win against Pitt, as Staubach completed all eight of his passes for 192 yards, Lawrence Robinson of the *New York World Telegram & Sun*, one of the nation's foremost college football writers, called him "probably the most talented quarterback in Navy history." Praise such as that, particularly emanating from the nation's media capital where all praise becomes bigger than life, began to thrust him into the national limelight.

He built on his new reputation during a close 13–6 loss to eventual national champion Southern California, and had not fullback Pat Donnelly lost a fumble as he was crossing the goal line late in the game, the Mids might have sprung the upset of the year. An entire nation was now aware that a young Navy quarterback was capable of doing some wondrous things on a gridiron. He had blistered the Trojans defense for 219 yards and tormented it with his running, including 18 yards for

Navy's only touchdown. Taking note of Staubach's astounding play, Southern Cal coach John McKay noted afterward, "What hurt us was not the plays they had worked on, but the ones when he was trapped." Roger was so impressive that the West Coast football writers ignored their own players and chose him as Pacific Coast Back of the Week.

Two weeks later, Staubach put on a performance of a lifetime, and a national audience watched openmouthed as he led underdog Navy to a stunning 34–14 victory over Army. The Cadets that year were coached by Paul Dietzel, who had won a national championship in 1958 at Louisiana State with a three-team mix that he called the White Team, the Go Team, and a primarily defensive unit called the Chinese Bandits.

Dietzel carried the gimmick to West Point, and the Chinese Bandits were so popular that a huge Chinese gong was rung and a few bars of Oriental music from the Army band accompanied their entry into a game. The cadets in the stands welcomed them by donning coolie hats and wore them for as long as the Bandits were on the field.

But no one could ever out-gimmick Hardin. He had his equipment people paint a small skull and crossbones on the front of the players' helmets, in honor of the *Jolly Roger*—not Staubach but the phantom ship of Navy lore that never lost a battle. As a talisman against the Chinese Bandits, a midshipman of Japanese descent provided the characters that said, "Beat Army." He sent a copy to his mother, but she wrote back and said he had made a mistake with one of the symbols and provided the correct one. Ever a stickler for detail, and not wanting to spoil this delicious gimmick, Hardin had all the stencils changed and replaced with the correct symbols.

Out in the fleet, the nuclear submarine USS *Grouper* patrolled with "Beat Army" painted on its hull; and Hardin predicted that his team would beat Army by an even bigger margin than the Mids' 43–12 victory in 1959 when Joe Bellino had such a great day and launched his bid for the Heisman Trophy.

Hardin was wrong on the score—but not by much—and this time it was Staubach who thrust himself into the following season's Heisman race with a stunning performance. He completed 10 of 12 passes for 204 yards and two touchdowns. He was Navy's leading rusher with 14 carries, many on his patented scrambling, and scored twice on runs of 21 and 2 yards. He astounded the sold-out crowd of 102,000 in Philadelphia's Municipal Stadium—including Navy's No. 1 fan, President John F. Kennedy—and millions watching on television with his spectacular style of play.

Army believed it could handle Staubach's running and passing. The Cadets had concluded their final practice at West Point with a symbolic sacking of the Navy quarterback as 14 seniors took shots at a tackling dummy outfitted with Staubach's jersey No. 12. In the game, they hardly ever got close to him, though it is doubtful that anyone watching on that balmy early December Saturday ever would have guessed that he was so nervous and excited that he barely slept the night before the game.

He ended a 63-yard drive with a spectacular 21-yard touchdown run in which every Army defender had a shot at him and he eluded all of them. Early in the second half, he sidestepped a couple of Army pass rushers and threw a little check-off pass that fullback Nick Markoff turned into a record-setting 65-yard touchdown for a 22–6 lead; and he climaxed this wondrous day by ending a fourth quarter, 89-yard drive with his second touchdown run.

After the game, Dietzel summed up what most coaches who faced Staubach had experienced themselves: "Four or five times, I thought we had him for a 20-yard loss. But always he seemed to wind up with a 15-yard gain. He's a really good football player—in fact, he's incredible."

And what of the Chinese Bandits? When they made their first appearance to the usual Oriental accompaniments, complete with coolie hats worn by the entire Corps of Cadets, the huge crowd was amused. Then it was stunned. In the age of potential cold war conflicts being framed at the time in the South China Sea over the islands of Quemoy and Matsu, the Midshipmen began waving miniature American flags. A rollicking cheer engulfed the stadium, and its salvo buried Army's well-publicized "new spirit" like a million guns barking across the field. The coolie hats quietly were put away, a fit metaphor for the fate of the Bandits and the rest of Army's team that day.

Later, Staubach confided to a friend, "I dreamed of such a day, but I never thought it could happen."

The Staubach mystique continued to grow at the Naval Academy away from the football field. Navy's basketball coach Ben Carnevale invited Staubach, who had been an all-city player in Cincinnati, to join his team as a guard. When Army came to the Naval Academy for its annual game, Staubach was assigned to guard the Cadets' best player, Joe Kosciusko, who was averaging almost 12 points a game. Carnevale told Roger to meet Kosciusko "at the locker room door, belly button to belly button." Carvnevale later revealed that he also had a secondary motive to the matchup: he wanted to remind the Army players of how Staubach and Navy had whipped them so decisively just three months earlier.

Staubach held Kosciusko to just six points in the first half and forced him to the bench for the rest of the game. Staubach didn't score a point, but Navy upset Army 55–48. After the game, Major General William C. Westmoreland, superintendent of the Military Academy, confronted the Navy coach.

"Damn it, Carnevale," he said, "Staubach's no basketball player."

"No sir," the Navy coach agreed, "but he's a winner."

Roger also excelled on the baseball field. He hit .410 as a sophomore and over .300 in his junior year while playing center field. During his senior year, he suffered a hamstring injury that was so severe, he couldn't even run to first base. But in a game against bitter neighborhood rival Maryland, coach Joe Duff summoned him as a pinch hitter with the tying and winning runs on base, and he hit a game-winning double.

Athletics weren't the only influence on Staubach's life at the Naval Academy, and none was greater than the Academy's Roman Catholic chaplain, Rev. Joseph Ryan. Roger served Mass for him several times a week ("he was the best one we had," Ryan said later) during his four years at the Naval Academy.

"He knew everyone on our team at Navy, and he was particularly close to the Catholic players because he saw them at Mass every week," Staubach said. "He loved sports, and he'd be at football practice as well as all the games."

Ryan, a native of Boston, was a football player on Fordham University's 1941 Sugar Bowl team when World War II broke out and he wanted to enlist in the marines immediately. One of the Jesuit priests at Fordham counseled him that he could serve both God and his country by becoming a military chaplain. So after the Rams defeated Missouri 2–0 in the Sugar Bowl, he left Fordham and entered the priesthood. World War II had ended when he was ordained, but he joined the Navy and served aboard the aircraft carrier USS *Oriskany* during the Korean War and had other shipboard assignments before coming to the Naval Academy in 1961.

Ryan and Staubach met again when both served in Vietnam. Roger was a supply officer at Da Nang, and Ryan was in the field with the marines where he often said Mass atop a bunker, on the hood of an armored vehicle, or atop a bunch of crates strung together to form an altar.

"We managed to keep in touch. He'd call me when he was out in the field with the marines," Staubach said. "Later, we were at Pensacola together, and our friendship grew to the point where he was like a surrogate father to me. He never ceased to display his heroism in the service of God and his country. He was wounded twice, and on one of those occasions, his server, George Pace, was killed instantly when a piece of shrapnel tore through his heart. It happened on July 4, 1967, and Father Ryan fulfilled a promise he made to the dead marine's family that he would say Mass for him on that date for as long as he lived."

Ryan was not unlike Rev. John "Jake" Laboon, who succeeded him as the Academy's Catholic chaplain. Laboon, a strapping 6'2", 200 pounder, played end for Navy in 1942 and 1943 and was an all-East selection in his senior season. He also was an All-American player on Navy's national champion lacrosse team in 1943. He had once earned the nickname "Sleepy" Laboon, a takeoff on a popular song of the day, "Sleepy Lagoon," after being led, wobbly legged, off the field during a scrimmage against the NFL champion Chicago Bears. (College and pro teams often engaged in scrimmages during this time.)

During World War II, he served aboard the submarine USS *Peto* and won the Silver Star for rescuing a downed navy flyer who was stranded on a reef. Laboon dove off the sub, swam to the reef, and then towed the airman to safety aboard the submarine while Japanese planes strafed him and his boat. That scene later was repeated in a movie starring John Wayne, where Wayne replicated Laboon's heroism.

After the war, Laboon resigned from the navy and later was ordained a Jesuit priest. He returned to the Naval Academy as a chaplain just as Ryan was leaving, and for the next quarter century, "Sleepy" Laboon was known as "Father Jake" to millions of navy and marine personnel. As Joe Ryan did, he served on the ground with the marines in Vietnam and earned the Legion of Merit with a combat "V." He also was the first chaplain assigned to a ballistic missile submarine squadron and he was fleet chaplain of the Atlantic Fleet before retiring. He later was stationed at a Jesuit retreat house just outside Annapolis and helped coach Navy's lightweight football team. Today, the frigate USS *John E. Laboon* sails in harm's way as part of a U.S. Navy fleet.

The heroism displayed by Ryan and Laboon demonstrates that valor on the battlefield is not limited only to those who carry guns. In World War I, Lieutenant William Davitt, a Catholic chaplain who had been a star on the 1906 and 1907 football teams at Holy Cross College in Worcester, Massachusetts, died in a bombing attack at the front lines in France, just 90 minutes before the armistice that ended the war was signed.

No one was more heroic than Rev. George Snavely Rentz, who had played football at Gettysburg College just prior to World War II. He became a minister, and during the war, a ship on which he was sailing was torpedoed, and he scrambled aboard a makeshift raft with several other survivors. Seeing that the raft was woefully overcrowded, he volunteered to leave so others had a better chance of survival. Twice his raftmates pulled him back from the sea, but when he left the raft a third time, he disappeared for good in the oily waters. The others on the raft all were rescued.

157

Throughout the 1962 season, it was evident to Hardin that Staubach was uncomfortable being harnessed into a disciplined drop-back passing system. But before the 1963 season, Hardin, a brilliant offensive coach who was not so foolishly stubborn as to try and rein in a talent like Staubach, devised an option system that combined Staubach's great mobility with the coach's drop-back beliefs. It was the best of both worlds as far as Hardin was concerned, and it turned out to be the best thing that could have happened to Staubach's offensive skills.

When the team was preparing to go to training camp at Quonset Point Naval Air Station in Rhode Island in mid-August, an informational flyer, *Meet Roger Staubach*, was sent to the thousand sportswriters around the nation who voted for the Heisman Trophy. It was the brainchild of Navy's creative athletic publicity director, L. Budd Thalman, and the first time that any school had pushed the nation's sportswriters to vote for a specific player even before the season began.

Staubach reveled in the challenge of the season, and not only because he was being linked to the Heisman Trophy. No one ever responded better to the pressures that accrue under such conditions than he did. How else can one explain all the miracle finishes that he orchestrated in college and professional football? He was that unique kind of player who was at his best when it was most important for him to win.

"He had all the qualities you find in a great person and a great leader," said Lynch, who was a splendid leader himself for one of the Naval Academy's greatest

U.S. Naval Academy Archives

Captain Tom Lynch (No. 51), shown here returning an interception, later became superintendent of the Naval Academy.

teams. "We responded to that, plus his coolness and his belief that he could always lead us to a win. Pretty soon, we started to believe it too, and that made us better. When we had the ball, our motto was 'Every block counts, and maybe three or four after that,' because he would be scrambling about, trying to dodge tacklers and find an open receiver. We wanted to give him every chance to make a play, and more often than not, he did."

Navy and Staubach started the season as predicted, with decisive victories over West Virginia and William & Mary. In the latter game, he set a school record with 297 total yards, and then broke it the following week with 307 yards in a 26–13 victory over Michigan as a national television audience looked on. He was never better, and that game, more than any other, gave him the credibility he needed to challenge for the Heisman Trophy. He accounted for three of his team's four touchdowns and in the process destroyed Michigan's pass defense by completing 14 of 16 passes for 237 yards.

His first touchdown came on arguably the most exciting five-yard run in college football history as he escaped from six tacklers while bobbing and weaving his way into the end zone. Later, just six seconds before the first half ended, it appeared he would hand off the ball to fullback Pat Donnelly and allow time to expire. Instead, he faked the run and then threw a 54-yard touchdown pass to Johnny Sai. "I have always believed he and John made up that play," Lynch said. "It wasn't like Roger to settle for three running plays when there was a chance to score a touchdown."

159

He also produced what has always been considered the quintessential Staubach play. Trying to pass, he had backpedaled, weaved, dodged, and scrambled backward until he was 19 yards behind the line of scrimmage. Two tacklers finally cornered him, and as he was going down, he managed to throw a 20-yard pass that netted just one yard. After the game, one of Navy's offensive linemen, explaining the play, noted, "You never block just once for Roger. You hit one man, then you get up and keep hitting people because he may take a little time back there."

"It was easy to win," Lynch noted, "when you had someone like that. We'd just say, 'Roger, score us another touchdown.'"

Even when the Mids lost their only game on the schedule—32–28 to Southern Methodist the following week—Staubach almost pulled out a win in the final second as his desperate pass to Skip Orr in the end zone was juggled and then knocked away by an SMU defender. During the game, he received a cheap shot in the back after making a handoff and had to leave the game. He returned a bit later and, forgetting about his injured shoulder, he ran five yards for a touchdown. After examining his shoulder the next day, doctors feared he might require surgery and have to miss the rest of the season. But they rigged a shoulder harness for him to wear, and he helped beat Virginia Military Institute the following week. It was not the Staubach of the first four weeks, but one who had to protect his shoulder, lest it pop out of its socket and end his season.

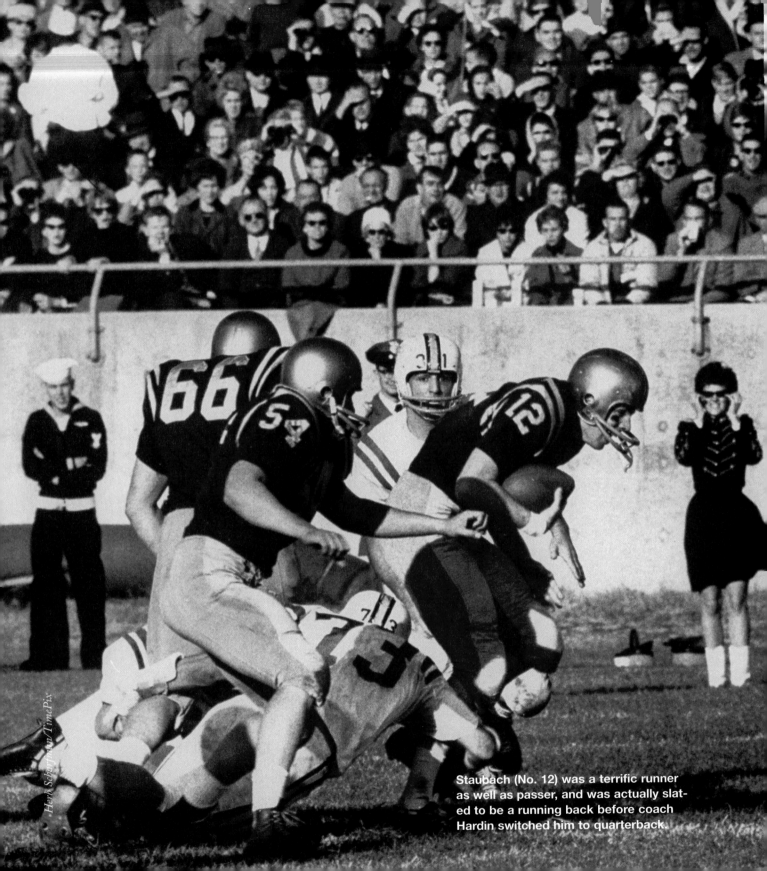

Staubach (No. 12) was a terrific runner as well as passer, and was actually slated to be a running back before coach Hardin switched him to quarterback.

Navy and Staubach easily handled two other tough opponents, Pitt and Notre Dame, before it played Army. Against unbeaten and third-ranked Pitt, Staubach rose to the challenge of determining which team would be ranked No. 1 in the East by leading Navy to a decisive 24–14 victory. A record-setting crowd at Navy–Marine Corps Stadium in Annapolis and a huge television audience watched in awe as he completed 14 of 19 passes and scored a touchdown—and took a giant step closer to the Heisman Trophy with his great overall performance.

The following week, he nailed down the Heisman at Notre Dame. The teams were tied 7–7 at halftime. Lynch told Staubach to leave the locker room, and then he told the team in no uncertain terms that it had to get going because a loss to Notre Dame would damage Roger's chances for a Heisman Trophy. The Mids settled down in the second half, and Staubach threw three touchdown passes in a 35–14 romp.

Navy finished its pre-Army season with two more wins. One of them was against Duke, and Lynch recalls a play where Staubach called a fake dive to fullback Pat Donnelly, and then he dropped back to jump pass the ball on a screen play to a running back. "But Duke covered the receiver, and three defenders closed in on him," Lynch recalled. "He shook loose from them and ran 45 yards, through diving Duke players. He had the sixth sense that all great players possess in that he always knew where trouble was coming from, and then he knew how to avoid it."

161

Herb Scharfman/TimePix

Navy's creative athletic publicity director, L. Budd Thalman, began touting Staubach as a Heisman Trophy candidate before the 1963 season.

Just as happened to Army's Pete Dawkins and Navy's Bellino a few seasons earlier, Heisman fever ran rampant because of Staubach's overall appeal. He had become a truly national figure with a cover story in *Time* magazine and two other national publications were preparing cover stories to coincide with the Army-Navy game. The Naval Academy tried to control the blizzard of media and personal appearance requests that were deluging Thalman's office while realizing there was no way to totally insulate an athlete of Staubach's caliber. Yet when he was approached

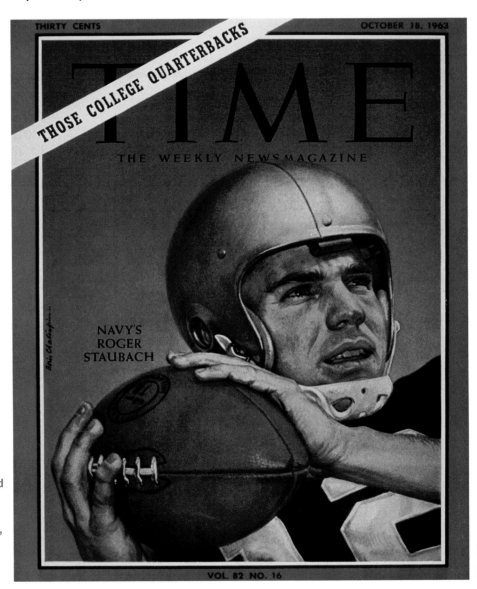

THIRTY CENTS

OCTOBER 18, 1963

THOSE COLLEGE QUARTERBACKS

TIME

THE WEEKLY NEWSMAGAZINE

NAVY'S
ROGER
STAUBACH

VOL. 82 NO. 16

TimePix

In mid-October, little more than a month before the nation was plunged into grief with the assassination of President Kennedy, Staubach made the cover of *Time* magazine.

after a game, he patiently answered all questions, signed scores of autographs, and posed for picture after picture.

At one point during the season, he kept asking Thalman for copies of his posed-action publicity picture. Thalman finally discovered that he was answering his own fan mail, sending out autographed pictures and paying for the postage himself. "We practically had to force him to bring the mail to our office," Thalman said. "There were several boxes filled with letters that he'd been tackling in what little spare time he had."

And then, in the midst of all the Heisman hoopla, on November 22, 1963, eight days before the Army game, everything came apart when president John F. Kennedy was assassinated in Dallas.

Like everyone else who heard the news on that day, the memory of it still is frozen in Staubach's memory:

"I was in my room in Bancroft Hall, getting ready to go to my thermodynamics class when I heard a commotion in the hall. I walked out to see what was happening, and someone yelled, 'Hey, the president's been shot.' I couldn't believe what I had just heard and asked again. It was the same message, 'The president's been shot.'

"When I got to class, the instructor was somewhere listening to a radio so everyone just sat and stared in total disbelief. He finally came in and told us the

163

AP/Wide World Photos

President Kennedy had become close to the football team in 1962 and 1963 at the Quonset Point Naval Air Station in Rhode Island.

One of the images
of a nation in
mourning etched
forever in the
memories of those
old enough to
recall them.

164

AP/Wide World Photos

president was dead. Sensing how crushed all of us were, he said he was going to stay in the classroom but we were free to do what we wanted. The mourning cycle started.

"I went over to the practice field and before too long, all the players had assembled, just standing around and numb with disbelief. The first thing coach Hardin did was have us kneel down and say a prayer. Then everything came to a halt. He didn't know if there would be a game against Army, and if there was, when it would occur. There was nothing we could do but wait, and it was during that time that the fine edge we had achieved throughout the season seemed to change."

Kennedy's death was a hammer blow to the Navy team. He was a naval officer and hero during World War II, commanding the famed motor torpedo boat, PT-109. When his boat was sunk by a Japanese destroyer, he swam ashore, though badly injured, to get help to rescue his crew.

Kennedy had quietly adopted the team after attending its preseason training base in 1962 and 1963 at Quonset Point Naval Air Station in Rhode Island. He used the base to transfer from *Air Force One* to a helicopter that took him to his summer White House on Cape Cod. He would stop by and often spent time with the team, watching them practice or meeting with the players. Before the 1962 Army-Navy game, he sent the team a telegram: "As president, I can't choose sides but I hope to be on the winning side of the field at the end of the game." He sat on Navy's side of the field in the second half of its 34–14 victory.

On November 26, 1963, four days after Kennedy's assassination, Staubach became the first junior since Army's Doc Blanchard in 1945, and only the second ever, to win the Heisman Trophy. There was no denying his credentials. He had led his team to a No. 2 national ranking while completing 101 of 150 passes for 1,375 yards and seven touchdowns. He had also run for another 363 yards. The same day, the Pentagon announced that the Army-Navy game would be played a week later than scheduled, at the request of President Kennedy's family, and in his honor.

Staubach's teammates celebrated his trophy in the locker room and threw him into the shower. But that was it. *Life* magazine, still the nation's top weekly, pulled back an issue featuring Staubach on its cover in favor of a picture of the slain president.

Herb Scharfman/TimePix

165

Life magazine, the nation's top weekly, pulled back a cover featuring Staubach in favor of a picture of the slain president.

"It was a terrible two weeks," Staubach said. "When the game was rescheduled, and we began to practice, that lifted everyone's spirits somewhat because we all wanted to play Army. Rescheduling the game was the right thing to do, but we carried a dual emotional burden of getting ready to play our foremost rival and still mourning not only the president, but a special friend.

"The players pretty much kept their emotions inside, but all of us were consumed by the tragedy. In the Yard, there wasn't any of the usual pre-Army-Navy-game hoopla, no huge bonfire, no banners nor signs. The famed statue of the Indian chief Tecumseh, always brightly painted before the game, had been scrubbed clean. There was just a single pep rally the night before the team left for Philadelphia. The signal being sent was, 'Just play the game, but play it well.'

"So when it came time to play, everything that had been pent up for two weeks inside of us just exploded. We just let everything go, and it led to a very good game."

Very good? The game became one for the ages. It was almost an exact replay of the famed 1946 game when an unbeaten Army team, featuring Doc Blanchard and Glenn Davis in their final game, barely made it through a 21–18 victory because 18-point underdog Navy ran out of time to run one final play from the Cadets' 3-yard line.

This time, Navy was the overwhelming favorite, despite Army's fine 7–2 record.

The Mids were ranked second in all the national polls and were being touted to play in the Cotton Bowl against national champion Texas—at that time, polls were determined only on regular-season games, and Texas had been picked No. 1 in the final poll—and the winner would declare itself national champion. But the Cotton Bowl invitation was contingent on Navy winning. If Army won, the Cadets would be invited, and Navy would go elsewhere. While the result wouldn't change the official national rankings, there were huge bragging rights at stake.

Most of the 102,000 fans who jammed Municipal Stadium had come to watch Staubach perform his magic, but on this day he had to share the spotlight with Carl Stichweh, Army's totally unheralded junior quarterback. Stichweh seemed to do everything for which Staubach was famous, and this became the key element in turning this game into one of the true classics of this renowned series.

The key to defeating Navy and Staubach was to keep Roger off the field so he couldn't work his magic. That's what Army tried to do. Stichweh used every second of the clock before the ball was snapped. His clever ball handling kept Navy's defense off balance and allowed Army's running backs to maintain possession of the ball for long periods of time. But the Cadets failed to take advantage of their opportunities and, save for an opening touchdown drive, they didn't score again until the fourth quarter when Navy led 21–7.

Staubach did the most with what he got—he had just five possessions in the entire game, less than half of Navy's usual total, but he drove the Mids to three touchdowns. With so little work, his numbers were modest—he threw 9 completions in 11 attempts for 99 yards, and he ran for another 55 yards. He flashed some

Staubach was nicknamed the "Dodger" because of his great open-field running and ability to elude tacklers.

of his magic on Navy's first scoring drive, passing for 27 yards to Johnny Sai on a fourth-down play, and he led a magnificent 93-yard drive for Navy's final touchdown, which ended when fullback Pat Donnelly scored the last of his record-tying three touchdowns for a 21–7 lead with 11 minutes to play.

It seemed that Navy had secured a win, but Staubach and his team never got on the field again and almost lost the game. He watched helplessly from the sidelines while Stichweh took over. First, Stichweh drove Army to a touchdown and then ran for a two-point conversion to close the gap to 21–15 with more than six minutes to play. He then joined Army's "hands" kickoff return team, and when the Cadets surprised Navy with a squib kickoff, Stichweh recovered the loose ball right in front Staubach, who was standing on the sidelines, ready to go back into the game.

Stichweh relentlessly drove his team toward Navy's end zone, chewing up the clock as he went. On fourth down at Navy's 23-yard line, he crossed up Navy's defense with a brilliant ball fake and lofted a pass to running back Don Parcells that gave the Cadets a first down at the 7-yard line, with 98 seconds to play.

On Navy's sideline, Staubach and Hardin planned their strategy if Army scored and took the lead. "It soon dawned on us that we weren't going to get the ball back, and if we did, there wouldn't be any time to do anything with it," Staubach said. "All we could do then was watch and hope that the defense could come up with a big play to kill Army's drive."

The stadium had become a seething cauldron of noise, and that became as big an obstacle for Stichweh as Navy's defense was. Each time he lined up to start a play, the noise thundered down on him, and he would ask referee Barney Finn to quiet the crowd so his signals could be heard by his team. Finn would stop the clock momentarily, raise his hand for quiet, and, when the din abated, restart the clock and Stichweh could run his play.

Three plays brought Army to Navy's 2-yard line. With 20 seconds left, the Cadets rushed to run their final play, and the crowd noise hit another crescendo. Stichweh again asked Finn to quiet the crowd. The referee raised his hands, and the clock was stopped. Unaccountably, Stichweh took his team back into a huddle and didn't notice Finn restarting the clock.

The huge crowd began chanting the final seconds, alerting the Cadets that the clock was running. They rushed to the line of scrimmage with eight seconds left, still enough time to run a play. The crowd noise reached another frenzy, and Stichweh again asked Finn for quiet. But the referee, totally frustrated by the continued requests, did nothing—and neither did Army as the clock ticked off its final seconds.

Two yards behind the line of scrimmage, Navy team captain and linebacker Tom Lynch clicked off the seconds in his mind; when he reached "two," he darted to the line and scooped up the ball just as linesman Ray Barbuti, who kept the time on the field, ran in from the sideline, yelling, "It's over, it's over."

"Stichweh told me later that he was exhausted during that drive. He had been on the field most of the game, he ran the ball, and now he was trying to cope with the noise and work without any timeouts," Staubach said. "He lost his focus and evidently forgot that when he asked the referee to quiet the crowd, the clock was stopped only until the ref thought it was quiet enough to resume play. Then it was restarted. Somehow, he thought the clock would not start again until the ball was snapped."

Thus ended one of the greatest games in the century-old Army-Navy series, made even more unique by all the events that had preceded it for two weeks and the presence of an extraordinary player like Staubach. On that rare day, his great talent and penchant for producing electrifying plays was limited, but he did what great players have always done—he found a way to lead his team to victory.

A week later, Staubach received his Heisman Trophy at the Downtown Athletic Club in New York City from Robert Wagner, mayor of New York City. Roger told those at the lavish awards dinner, "I wish I could cut this into 44 pieces and give one to every member of the team, because without them I never could have won it." He was besieged with requests for media interviews; he appeared on the famed Ed Sullivan television show during which he had the stoic Sullivan in convulsions with a prearranged, under-the-chin wave to his buddies back at the Naval Academy; and then came even more national honors, including the Maxwell Award.

But not everyone knew who he was, at least not in person. The evening before the Heisman presentation, Staubach attended a Broadway show dressed in his Midshipman's uniform. He stood in the theater's entrance awaiting his parents and future wife, Marianne. "Because of my uniform, people thought I was an usher and kept handing me their tickets," he recalled. "That experience kept me pretty humble."

Of course, his season wasn't finished because Navy went to the Cotton Bowl, but it was soundly beaten by Texas, 28–6. Staubach set a Cotton Bowl record by completing 21 of 31 passes for 228 yards. But the game was lost even before it began when the team's unity, which had been such an integral part of its success that season, became unraveled. "When we got to Dallas a week before the game, some of the players, most of whom hadn't played very much and weren't apt to see any action in this game, started grumbling about a bunch of stuff, like having to give up a week's Christmas leave, and there was a disconnect that we didn't have all season," Staubach said. "Our captain Tom Lynch finally got everyone together and said, 'Hey, this is a chance of a lifetime. What are a couple of days leave?'

"We played well after getting behind 14–0, but it was almost impossible catching up against a great team like Texas. Added to that, Pat Donnelly, our fullback and linebacker, injured his hamstring, and that cost us our running game and negated his mobility on defense. Texas used it to its great advantage."

In 1964, every football expert in the nation predicted that Staubach could become the first two-time winner of the Heisman Trophy. But there was no way they could have predicted the misfortunes that befell him and Navy's team with an almost unending spate of injuries to key players, Staubach and Donnelly being foremost.

Roger suffered a severe ankle injury in the season's opening game, a victory over Penn State, and its effects cost him playing time and severely hampered his mobility for the rest of the season. The ankle was so bad that Hardin decided not to

College Football Hall of Fame

Despite Staubach completing 21 of 31 passes for 228 yards, Navy lost to Texas 28–6 in the Cotton Bowl. Getting ready to receive the handoff from Staubach is No. 48 John Sai.

play him in the second game against William & Mary. But the Mids had only a 14–6 lead midway through the final quarter, and Hardin sent him into the game. It was like old times. On the first play, he handed the ball to halfback Kip Paskewich, who ran 76 yards for a TD. On his next possession, Roger threw a touchdown pass to John Mickelson, and Navy went on to win 35–6.

That was the last of the good news until his final appearance at Navy–Marine Corps Stadium against Duke. In that game, he broke his Naval Academy single-game total-offense record with 308 yards, completing 21 of 30 passes for 217 yards, and he ran 17 times for 91 yards.

In his final game against Army, he showed one last brilliant flash of the real Staubach on a two-point conversion that tied the score, 8–8, at halftime. He scrambled about trying to find an open receiver before one Army tackler grabbed his legs and another reached for his passing arm. He switched the ball to his left hand, and, as he was going down, he returned it to his right hand and threw it nearly 15 yards into the end zone where end Phil Norton leaped to make the catch.

That was his final, shining moment. Navy lost 11–8, its first loss to Army in six games. After the two teams saluted their fans with the traditional playing of their alma maters, hordes of joyful cadets and Army rooters swarmed over the field. In the midst of the throng, Staubach walked off the field, alone and almost unnoticed. There would be no second Heisman Trophy, and in its place there was the acrid taste of defeat.

Nearly 40 years later, the loss still bothered him, though he had done everything possible to try and rally a team ravaged by injury—a mere shell of the one that had so captivated the nation just a year earlier.

"I've always believed that I should have figured out a way to get us a win," Staubach said. "Army scored just 11 points, and there had to be some way that I could have gotten us more than 11 points. I've always been disappointed in myself for not doing that."

What he did accomplish, though, was very impressive, establishing career records at that time for total offense (4,253 yards), completions (463), and passing yardage (3,571). He won seven varsity letters in football, baseball, and basketball. At the 1965 graduation, he won the Naval Academy Athletic Association Sword, given to the outstanding senior athlete, and his third straight Thompson Trophy Cup, given to the overall athlete of the year. In a rare tribute, matched only by a similar one when Bellino graduated four years earlier, the Brigade of Midshipmen asked that his jersey No. 12 be retired. He broke down and wept when he was called back on stage and presented with the jersey.

The brigade, also aware of his deep religious faith, gave him a very personal gift—a pair of religious rosary beads that were blue and gold, the Navy colors and those of the Blessed Virgin Mother for whom the beads are dedicated.

Staubach's football career lingered on in two All-Star games immediately after the 1964 season: the North-South and the East-West, where he was chosen most valuable player; the following August, he played in the College All-Star Game against the defending NFL champion Cleveland Browns. He badly reinjured his shoulder early in that game and finally had it repaired for good back at the Naval Academy.

All Navy football players know that the sport is only a temporary respite before their real career begins—serving their country. Some, like Bellino and Staubach and other stars before and after them, served their first six months as plebe coaches. But once that ended, their only duty was the serious business of defending their country, a job where gridiron exploits mean nothing.

It has been that way ever since Abertus Catlin, captain of Navy's 1889 team, became a marine officer and was cited for bravery as commander of the marine detachment aboard the USS *Maine* when it was blown up in Havana harbor. He also was commended for bravery during the landings at Vera Cruz in 1914 during the so-called Punitive Expedition when U.S. forces fought the bandits who were harassing the states abutting Mexico. Three former Navy players—future coach and athletic director Jonas Ingram, who played in 1903–1906; Allen Buchanan, from the 1898 team; and Fred McNair, who played in 1900–1903—were awarded the Medal of Honor for bravery during that campaign. Catlin, as a brigadier general during World War I, died from wounds incurred while leading his troops in the battle of Belleau Woods in France.

Even men such as Johnny Poe, a civilian and a descendant of author Edgar Allen Poe, who coached football at the Naval Academy in 1896, are included in the list. Poe was a colorful character, a real-life model for the fictional stories written about the last days of Western frontier life in America at the end of the 19th century. A member of the famed Poe family that sent six coaches into collegiate football at that time, he was paid $501.25 to coach Navy in 1896, but he disdained an invitation to return in 1897. He was a restless young adventurer who preferred the rough and tumble of the West to standing on the sidelines. Before he reached his 25th birthday he became a folk hero of sorts with what amounted to a lifetime of incredible adventures.

He was a mounted police officer in the Nevada mining camps; he single-handedly caught a gang of cattle rustlers; he "thrashed" a man who had insulted the American flag; he became a folk hero by helping to round up a gang of robbers in Death Valley after they had robbed a Wells Fargo office. He was a member of the survey team that set the very narrow boundary between the United States, British Columbia, and Alaska. He fought in Cuba during the Spanish-American War and joined the U.S. Army in the Philippines. He was killed during World War I as a member of Britain's famed Black Watch Guards.

Heroism by former Navy players also took on different forms. Richard Evelyn Byrd Jr. was small and wiry, but he also was a tough, able athlete who was a wrestling champion at the Academy in 1912. He was a backup quarterback for four years, battling a series of injuries that hampered his career. But he never gave up, just as he persevered when he and chief machinist mate Floyd Bennett were the first to over-fly the North Pole, for which they were awarded the Medal of Honor. Two years

U.S. Naval Academy Archives

Admiral Richard Byrd.

173

later, after establishing his Little America base camp in Antarctica, Byrd was the first to overfly the South Pole.

John Rogers was a three-year tackle at the turn of the century who, as a pioneer in Navy aviation, was designated naval aviator No. 2. Renowned for his fearlessness as a long-distance seaplane flier, he attempted one of the first transoceanic flights from San Francisco to Hawaii, as part of a three-plane group. Two of the planes turned back, and his plane later went off course because of faulty navigational gear. He ran out of fuel and landed in the Pacific Ocean, but instead of waiting to be rescued, he and his crewman, Lieutenant B. J. Connell, rigged a sail from the fabric of one of the plane's wings and "sailed" the plane nearly 450 miles to within 10 miles of Kauai before they were picked up. They were credited with a flight record of 1,841 miles that stood for five years.

Then there was "Jumpin' Joe" Clifton, a fine running back in the late twenties. His "football personality" was perfect for his career as a naval aviator because he was an extremely daring and competitive person. On night-flying training exercises, he often turned off his running lights so no one could see him performing his crazy acrobatic flying exercises.

During World War II, he commanded VF-12 as part of USS *Saratoga's* Air Group Twelve, which was commanded by Harold Caldwell, the man whose backfield position he inherited on Navy's football team. Clifton escorted Caldwell's bombers on raids in the Solomon Islands, and he won two Distinguished Flying Crosses for heroism. One of his most daring escapades occurred when he was ordered to train British pilots for combined air operations with navy pilots. He and another navy pilot flew their planes to the British aircraft carrier HMS *Illustrious*. As Clifton approached the flight deck, he could not locate the landing signal officer who would direct him in his landing. No worry. He simply landed without direction—any carrier landing is a tricky affair, and one without direction is almost beyond description—and once on deck, presented himself to a very startled British admiral who had no idea he had even arrived.

Staubach later had a terrific example of heroism in Tom Landry, his head coach with the Cowboys. As a 19-year-old bomber pilot during World War II, Landry was returning from his 25th and last mission before being sent back to the United States. But his plane was badly shot up during its mission over Germany and barely made it back to England. There, he had to crash-land it in a wooded field. Luckily, he was able to steer it between two trees, shearing off the wings. But he and his crew escaped without a scratch.

Staubach certainly had the personality suited to flying fighter aircraft or commanding a submarine because he was, by nature, daring and resourceful, and he always thought in terms of attacking the opposition. But that was precluded by his color blindness, of all things, a problem not detected by Navy doctors until after he was enrolled as a plebe.

One of the delicious ironies of Staubach's college career is that had it not been for a medical technician ignoring the malady during a physical examination, he would have been rejected at the Naval Academy. His regular eyesight was in the 20/15 or 20/10 range, but when it came to identifying a group of colored dots, he had problems. The seaman administering the tests when Staubach and his group showed up was comfortably ensconced in his chair with his feet propped up on the desk, and he was clearly bored with the whole procedure.

While Roger quickly ran through a group of charts with red, yellow, and green dots, the person standing behind him whispered, "You're missing some of those col-

Tom Landry.

AP/Wide World Photos

ors." When the test was finished, the seaman said, "Hey, you missed a couple, but that's not bad," and he gave Staubach a passing mark. That was the first and only time he ever passed a color test.

"You don't know whether it was fate or not," Staubach said. "It wasn't like I failed the test and then someone up the ladder said, 'That's Roger Staubach the quarterback, so we'll pass him.' The seaman just wasn't paying attention. Had he been paying strict attention and failed me, I wouldn't have gotten into the Naval Academy."

Indeed, when he took another medical exam at the Naval Academy, a doctor administered the color blindness test, and again Roger failed.

"How did you get in here?" the doctor asked him.

Had he not been granted admission, who knows how the Roger Staubach saga would have turned out? Most likely, it would have been just as great because Staubach had the rare ability of not only using his talents to surpass their potential but also of bringing along others to the same high levels.

But the color blindness affected his career as a naval officer because he could never go on line with duty at sea, where promotions and career advancements are richest; nor could he become a navy pilot. His options were the Marine Corps, civil engineering, and the supply corps. He considered service in the Marine Corps before choosing the supply branch. The marines had tried to recruit him to serve at Quantico where there was a very fine service football team. Many of his classmates acted like marines before they were marines—as midshipmen they exhibited all of the gung ho spirit for which the Corps was renowned. Staubach said that they even wore their combat boots while studying and marine fatigue caps walking around Bancroft Hall.

"I loved the Marine Corps and respected it, but if you wanted to be one when you went to the Naval Academy, then you did it without any hesitation," Staubach said. "But I didn't know what I wanted to be so I didn't think I fit into the Marine Corps."

After finishing supply school, he volunteered for duty in Vietnam where America had begun escalating its involvement in a civil war in which the Communist north was attempting to take over the south and begin a domino conquest of southeast Asia.

"I wanted to go because I believed that we . . . were doing the right thing—trying to stop the threat of communism in Southeast Asia," he wrote in his autobiography, *First Down, Lifetime to Go.* "Later the war became controversial and I saw things that I disagreed with and questioned. But at the time I went, I strongly felt I had my duty to do. So I chose shore duty in Vietnam for a year. That may have been the longest year of my life."

Staubach was well aware of the consequences of military combat. One of his two uncles who served in the army during World War II was a combat veteran, and a cousin was wounded in the Korean War. His father was ready to serve during World War II but was disqualified because he was diabetic. Roger could have escaped his commitment to the Naval Academy after he finished at New Mexico Military Institute because his scholastic achievements were good enough for acceptance at any university. But he kept his word, attending the Academy and then accepting without question the minimum four-year active duty commitment.

This foreclosed any immediate professional sports offers, particularly as a certain first-round draft pick given his collegiate record, in either the National Football League or the new American Football League. Because of that commitment, in the 1965 draft, Dallas made him a 10th-round pick, and the AFL's Kansas City Chiefs picked him in the 15th round. He eventually signed with the Cowboys, who paid him a $10,000 signing bonus and $500 a month during his navy career. He joined the team after he left the navy and became one of the greatest quarterbacks in NFL history.

As part of his preparatory training for Vietnam, Staubach went through a mock prisoner of war camp at Whitney Island, Washington. It was as realistic an experience as the navy could provide—based on what had been learned from Korean POW camps and bits of information gleaned from conditions in North Vietnamese camps. The guards even wore communist uniforms, and they did everything an American POW could expect, except hand out physical punishment.

While he got only a sample of the ordeals he was apt to face if ever captured by the communists, some of the experiences still make him wince, such as living in a black box no bigger than a television set for four or five hours while forced to be in a squatting position with his back bent forward. When they put him in an even smaller box, he said that he almost went berserk trying to break out—and he was there for only five minutes.

Yet, as you might expect of Staubach, he had a moment of triumph when he "escaped" by suddenly running from his guards, climbing over a barbed wire fence, and sprinting into nearby woods. The guards finally called him back, telling him he had made "a good escape." He used a jacket to shield his body from the jagged wire, but he cut his arms pretty badly and shredded some of his clothes. His triumph ended after an hour's rest when he had to resume his indoctrination.

While awaiting transportation to Vietnam, he lived with a couple of Navy SEALs, Eddie Gill and Larry Graham. He recalls them as being "young and fearless but I'm sure that after they had some action in Vietnam, they were like the rest of us—very aware of our mortality but still not afraid to do their jobs."

Staubach's first stop in South Vietnam was at Da Nang on the South China Sea. He was assigned to run a petroleum depot about six miles from the Da Nang base, replacing Lieutenant, Junior Grade, Andy Havola who had part of his arm accidentally shot off by one of his own men during a Vietcong raid the night before Staubach arrived.

"You could drive to the site without much fear during the day, but there were snipers along the road at night, and you weren't supposed to drive the route," Staubach said. "Andy got caught at the base after dark, and when sniper fire began, the marines were called to check it out. The navy guys had bunkers for security, but everyone was jittery, and that's when one of his own men accidentally shot him.

"I always downplayed the risk of any danger when I wrote to my wife, Marianne. When we were together in Honolulu on an R and R trip, there was a story in the local newspaper about the incident, and it mentioned that I had succeeded Andy and was back in Hawaii on R and R. I had never met Andy, but he was in Honolulu at the same time, read the article, and showed up at our hotel room to introduce himself as the man who I relieved.

"My wife looked at Andy, with part of an arm missing, then looked at me and said, 'So, you weren't in any danger, huh?'

177

"The truth is that you were in danger no matter where you were in Vietnam. I know guys were ambushed and killed in the villages around our base, but I was very fortunate that nothing happened to me."

Staubach also was in charge of receiving and shipping all the personal effects of servicemen killed in action. Seeing the body bags carrying the remains of soldiers and marines somehow convinced him that he wasn't contributing enough, and he asked to be transferred to a more responsible job. In an interview with the newspaper *Stars and Stripes*, he lamented the fact that he didn't think he was doing enough working in a support group like the supply corps.

"I got hammered for it, and rightly so because I was wrong," he said. "I was doing a job and everyone else over there was doing their job. So I got into trouble with everyone who was working in a support role for having denigrated our mission.

"Still, I have often wondered just how my life would have been affected if I had been with the marines in a combat situation."

He recalled an early morning mortar attack when he was stationed at Chu Lai, about 60 miles south of Da Nang. Mortar rounds are distinguished by a whistling sound after they begin their descent, followed by a dull explosion. Those are the only warning signals, and at the sound of the first whoomp when the round hit, everyone scrambled from their quarters and ran into bunkers. "We were never subjected to frontal attacks because we were surrounded by marines, but the mortar attacks were scary," he said. "You don't hear them coming until they are about to hit. We had a few people killed, which was like getting hit by lightning because they cannot be precisely aimed. Once you got into a bunker you were safe, but until then, you never knew where a round would land."

Even the relative safety of Da Nang did not insulate Staubach from the pangs of war when his Navy teammate and friend Tom Holden, a marine officer, was shot and killed as he charged over a hill while directing his platoon in a fire-fight against the Vietcong. Holden, an offensive guard and linebacker on the 1963 Cotton Bowl team, had come through Da Nang en route to an R and R locale and tried, but failed, to contact Roger and Fred Marlin, the captain of the 1964 team who was stationed nearby. They later had made plans to get together at the officer's club in Da Nang, but Holden was killed before it happened.

Staubach had several teammates who distinguished themselves in heroic actions after they graduated. End Jim Campbell was credited with saving many lives during a fire on the deck of the carrier USS *Constellation* after a rocket was accidentally fired and ran amok among planes and ammunition. Vern Von Sydow, a guard on the 1962 team, was a much-decorated helicopter pilot in Vietnam, and Bruce Bickel, who played quarterback behind Staubach, also distinguished himself in combat. Tom Lynch, captain of the 1963 team, became the superintendent of the Naval Academy.

Staubach was crushed when he heard about the brutal death of Mike Grammar, who was a friend during his plebe year at the Naval Academy. He was told

Admiral Tom Lynch.

179

that Grammar, a marine lieutenant, and a sergeant had been captured by the Vietcong, had their hands bound behind their backs, and then were executed. Added to that were stories he had heard of the kamikaze-style killings of unsuspecting marines and soldiers by alleged innocent villagers who were in fact Vietcong with explosives hidden on their bodies, and of booby-trapped huts that while being searched became death traps for the Americans. He understood then why the marines often were very aggressive when they entered villages, but always within the rules of engagement.

He also understood the tradition that says that there comes a time when one must make the supreme sacrifice. The ranks of Naval Academy graduates include many who gave their lives in combat or in situations that helped to save their comrades. There is no better example than Gus Lentz, a tackle and captain of the 1925 team. He died when the aircraft carrier USS *Wasp* was sunk during the battle of the eastern Solomons in 1942. Lentz, who weighed nearly 240 pounds, had been wounded earlier in the attack and lay in the ship's sick bay, unable to move. When the order was given to abandon the ship, he knew that his size would probably jam an escape route, thereby endangering the lives of other shipmates. So Lentz ordered the medical staff to leave him behind, and he perished with the ship.

At Chu Lai, Staubach was in charge of the freight terminal division that off-loaded and loaded cargo ships. The off-loading was precarious because the cargo generally was huge amounts of bombs and ammunition; the loading primarily involved removing body bags from 25 or 30 ambulances and placing them on ships returning to the United States. It was not an easy task, knowing that the contents had once been vibrant young men, most younger than himself, who willingly paid the supreme price in service to their country.

Added to that were feelings formed by his own experiences, the death of teammates and classmates such as Holden and Grammar, and the tales of communist atrocities in Korea, told to him by the commander of a detachment of South Korean marines who were stationed nearby. All of that, he admits, caused him to form some virulent feelings against the enemy in Vietnam.

Later, the lack of national leadership in Washington that was becoming evident on the battlefield, plus the constant flow of body bags and firsthand stories about American forces being hamstrung in fighting the enemy, caused him to question the manner in which American forces were involved. He saw the war as a right and just cause to save South Vietnam from the horrors of communism, but with the lack of a cohesive plan for winning, he agonized about Americans having died for no good reason.

It is very understandable how someone like Staubach, who knew only how to win and always did everything possible to try and make it happen, had such resentment.

He later wrote in *First Down, Lifetime to Go*: "The Vietnamese War was a screwed-up mess. Some of our allies, such as France, were sending supplies to our enemy. People in our own country were protesting the war and we weren't fighting the war as a war. It was like playing for a tie. We were allowed to fight to a certain point and then stop, whereas the enemy went all out.

"With our limited war policies, it was like sending a quarterback into a game with one arm tied behind his back. I know . . . it is easier to say that we should have escalated the war effort and gone all out to win. The tragedy, though, was sending our troops over there to fight and then limiting what they could do. If you ask a man to put his life on the line, you should let him have full maneuverability and give him all available weapons to defend himself."

Staubach gained even more fame as a quarterback when he starred for the Dallas Cowboys.

AP/Wide World Photos

Conferring on the sidelines with coach Tom Landry.

AP/Wide World Photos

182

Staubach left Vietnam in August 1967. He spent the next two years as a supply officer at Pensacola Naval Air Station in Florida and was able to resume his football career on the base team. His only involvement with the game in Vietnam was an occasional game of catch or a pickup touch game on a makeshift field he had constructed. He wore out a couple of footballs that the Cowboys had sent him, but it took him almost a full season of service football, playing mostly against smaller southern colleges, to reawaken the skills that had lain dormant since 1964. He left the Navy in July 1969 and immediately joined the Cowboys.

But he has never forgotten his roots at the Naval Academy or the experience he accumulated serving in the navy.

"When they introduced me before an NFL game, I was always proud to be referred to as, 'Roger Staubach, Navy.' I have a common denominator with people involved in a capital campaign at the Naval Academy. We all spent time there; we all had the same experiences there. Many of the people working on that campaign with me turned out to be my heroes in the service."

He also takes great pride in having done active duty, particularly the year he served in Vietnam. He has said many times that had it not been for the insatiable desire to play football, he most likely would have become a career officer. He also brushes aside any suggestions that he missed a lot in his professional football career by having to fulfill a four-year service obligation.

Staubach has
enjoyed a very
successful career
in business since
his playing days
ended.

183

"I did the best I could," he said, "and I would do it again. I had a big job in Chu Lai handling all the ammunition supplies which came through the port. I got close to a lot of marines there. I could have gone to Pensacola or Quantico right out of the Naval Academy, but I didn't want to spend my life playing service football. I only spent four years in the navy, but I did my job and I've never felt inadequate to say that I wasn't a career officer."

Most of all, he carries forever a great admiration for people who risk their lives for just causes.

"They are heroes in the truest sense of the word," he said. "Those firefighters in New York City went into buildings to save lives on 9/11. Those military guys now in Afghanistan are doing their job. Father Joe Ryan would say Mass in bunkers, knowing that he could be killed at any moment. You must be thankful that people care that much about you and me.

"I really learned to appreciate life after Vietnam. I also know how tough it is for Vietnam War veterans who were in the field to deal with the memories of seeing their buddies die or get their arms or legs shot off. It really ticks you off when people don't respect that these men were fighting for their country, whether or not they liked the war. Now we are seeing a reunification of our national spirit. But still a war is going on. We told those guys to go to Vietnam and they fought the enemy there and the opposition at home. Today, they can say, 'Thank God' for everyone being together as our forces are deployed to fight terrorism."

Chapter 5
Heisman Heroes on Other Fields

Winning the Heisman Trophy and engaging in military service certainly weren't limited to the quintet from the Military Academy and Naval Academy who won the award. Indeed, it seems that the Heisman is renowned for the number of its early winners who left behind all the glories of playing on the football field for the even-greater glories achieved in defense of their country on battlefields around the world.

The award was established in 1935, just as war clouds were beginning to form over Europe and the Far East. Five years later, this nation had begun mobilizing the mightiest military force ever to stop the aggression that was threatening to engulf the entire world. It continued to maintain those strong forces well into the first quarter century of Heisman Trophy winners. So it was not coincidental that they, like millions of other football players and nonplayers throughout the country, joined the nation's military. Many of them were decorated for valor in battle; one, Nile Kinnick of Iowa, the 1939 winner, died while on active duty as a navy carrier pilot.

Nine of the first thirteen winners were in the military during World War II; Davey O'Brien, the 1938 winner, was an agent for the FBI during this time; Frank Sinkwich, the 1942 Heisman winner from Georgia, joined the marines, but his legs were so battered from football that he was given a medical discharge after a year; 1944 winner Les Horvath served in the navy as a dentist after the war; and the 1945 and 1946 winners, Glenn Davis and Doc Blanchard, also did post–World War II duty. Blanchard was a member of the United States Air Force during the Korean War, and he flew 113 combat missions in southeast Asia, 84 of them over North Vietnam.

The 1947 winner, Johnny Lujack of Notre Dame (pictured on opposite page surrounded by fans), also was a naval officer during World War II, but he later played two seasons of college football before winning his Heisman Trophy.

Many of the winners following Lujack in the late forties and fifties also served in the military for varying lengths of time, but none of them were called to combat duty.

The World War II years of 1940–1945 so consumed the nation that its armed forces grew to more than 12 million by the time victory had been achieved. That placed a tremendous strain on leadership requirements, and one of the prime areas of recruitment was among college graduates and students. Of course, West Point and Annapolis played their usual key role in producing young combat officers. In 1942, following the attack on Pearl Harbor, which actively plunged America into the war, they shortened their curricula from four to three years. But that wasn't enough to satisfy the demand for leaders of smaller combat units in all the services, so the government established officer training programs, over and above the traditional

Frank Sinkwich.

Frank Sinkwich
University of Georgia

Downtown Athletic Club

Reserve Officers' Training Corps (ROTC) and navy ROTC models, at hundreds of colleges and universities throughout the nation.

A new factor had emerged apart from the conventional army and navy forces. The development of combat aircraft since World War I had drastically changed the manner in which war was waged, and the most critical need was for trained aviators. It was true for both the army air forces and the navy's greatly expanded air arm that had to provide pilots for the thousands of planes being flown off the rapidly expanding number of aircraft carriers.

Thus, it is no coincidence that six of the first eleven winners—Jay Berwanger, Clint Frank, Kinnick, Tom Harmon, Bruce Smith, and Blanchard—were aviators. The military had discovered that the foot skills of players, particularly running backs, who had to use their feet suddenly and decisively when making cuts on a football field, were well suited to working the foot pedals of the combat planes, particularly the fighter planes.

Berwanger, for example, was a naval aviator and pilot trained to land using only instruments in coordination with the plane's foot pedals. Frank, from Yale, was

187

Downtown Athletic Club

Jay Berwanger.

Clint Frank and teammate Larry Kelly.

drafted into the army in 1941, graduated from army air forces flight school, and served as an aide to General James Doolittle. He later became the executive officer of the 98th Bomb Group and flew combat missions in Africa, Italy, and western Europe. The latter was particularly harrowing duty because German air defense took a heavy toll on American bombers flying long-range missions without full fighter escort.

A great premium was placed on acquiring athletes like Berwanger and Frank, particularly by the navy preflight programs. They were developed under the direction of Commander Tom Hamilton, one of the Naval Academy's greatest football players from the mid-twenties, and later a pioneer in carrier-based aviation. Hamilton had also been a successful head coach for three years at the Naval Academy during the mid-thirties; and before and after this assignment, he had integrated his military assignments with further coaching duties with various navy ship and base teams.

This background was the perfect entrée to establish a system for training aviators, which he enlarged by having many college football coaches oversee the physical instruction portion of the preflight curriculum. Many of these instructors, augmented by outstanding college and professional players, became a who's who of great college coaches, including Jim Crowley, one of Notre Dame's famed Four Horsemen, who had guided Fordham to its glory days in the thirties; Jim Tatum, then at North Carolina; Dick Hanley from Northwestern; Don Faurot from Missouri; Bud Wilkinson, then coaching at Syracuse; and Paul "Bear" Bryant from Alabama. These programs were established in five major geographic areas around the country, and all of them fielded athletic teams that played against collegiate and service competition.

189

The program was as named—preflight, meaning that the enrollees did not learn to fly were given a curriculum that each day consisted of a morning devoted to technical subjects that were preparation for the navigation, bombing, and gunnery lessons yet to come at flight school and an afternoon engaged in a wide variety of physical exercise activities that were designed to increase and sharpen hand-eye-foot coordination.

The navy also established huge "V" officers' training programs at scores of colleges around the nation to handle the demands for ship and ground combat officers. Enrollees in these programs, both navy and marines, had regular college curricula augmented by some military subjects until called to active duty. Then they were sent to the various service schools for specific military instruction. Upon graduation, they were assigned to the fleet or marine combat divisions.

The army continued its ROTC program but in the early part of the war forbade its enrollees from participating in intercollegiate athletics. Thus, many from Ohio State's 1942 national championship team still were enrolled at the university in 1943 but could not play during that season. When the ban was lifted in 1944, several were members of the Buckeyes' unbeaten team that season, including Heisman Trophy winner Les Horvath, then enrolled in Ohio State's School of Dentistry.

Nile Kinnick.

Iowa's Nile Kinnick, who won the Heisman Trophy in 1939, is one of the all-time Cinderella stories, much like Pete Dawkins of Army was in 1958. He was not a physically imposing player, just five feet, eight and a half inches, and he weighed 170–175 pounds. He also was the slowest of Iowa's running backs. It was said that teammate Bill Green was a better runner and Roger Pettit was a better punter—but never in a game. Dr. Eddie Anderson, his coach during his Heisman season, once declared that "if Kinnick could run a 10-second 100-yard dash, the Big Ten would ban him."

Yet, his teammates and the student body at Iowa idolized him because he had a lot of the Dawkins qualities in him (or did Dawkins have a lot of Kinnick in him?). More than four decades after he died in a crash while trying to land his navy fighter plane on an aircraft carrier, his former teammates still held him in awe. They had voted him the team's most valuable player for the 1939 season, and the student body chose him as the school's athlete of the year. He had, they said, an aura of being someone special. The senior class at Iowa must have thought so too, because in 1939, it elected him to the School of Commerce's Order of Artus honor society; he won the Iowa Athletic Board Cup for excellence in scholarship and athletics; he was senior class president for the College of Liberal Arts; he was president of the senior class presidents of the 10 colleges and schools at Iowa.

191

Kinnick finished his undergraduate years with a 3.4 average and was one of just 30 students from a student body of 5,000 who was elected to Phi Beta Kappa.

He was the featured back, or tailback, in Iowa's offense—he ran, passed, kicked, and then played defense.

Kinnick was all–Big Ten in 1937, but playing with what many believed was a broken ankle throughout the 1938 season, he was just an average player as a junior. His 1938 team didn't score a point in its last five games, and its record during his first two seasons was 2–13–1. He was all but invisible on offense during the last five games of his junior year and didn't score a point.

So Kinnick wasn't on anyone's Heisman list when the 1939 season began. But Anderson, who had just finished a six-year head coaching stint at Holy Cross College in Massachusetts, with a gaudy 47–7–4 record, changed everyone's mind when he revamped the entire team. His football credentials were very worthy: he had been coached at Notre Dame by Knute Rockne and had played with George Gipp.

Anderson installed—as did everyone who ever played for Rockne—the Notre Dame box formation. The team never formed a huddle but lined up in a tight T formation from which the quarterback called the play and gave the snap count. The backs then did a quick shift to an alignment similar to the single wing, but the line stayed balanced. The play was run and the process repeated again, always at flank speed so opponents never had a chance to regroup.

Kinnick became a star with this system. Yet, it was his stamina—he played 402 consecutive minutes from the start of the season's second game until he had to leave the final game in the third quarter with a separated shoulder—as much as his great performances that astounded everyone. Anderson hung the tag "Ironmen" on him and his team, and it caught on across the country and kept him in the national spotlight. The team lost only to Michigan and the following year's Heisman winner, Tom Harmon, 27–7. It tied its final game against Northwestern, 7–7.

Kinnick flashed to national attention in Iowa's second game when he accounted for all of his team's scores in a 32–29 victory over Indiana. He ran for 103 yards and a touchdown, threw three touchdown passes, returned a kickoff 73 yards for a touchdown, and had a 22-yard average for nine punt returns.

Three weeks later, Iowa staged the upset of the year by defeating Notre Dame 7–6 as Kinnick scored the Hawkeyes' only touchdown with 40 seconds to play in the first half. He kicked the extra point and then kept the Irish at bay with a record 16 punts for a 45.6-yard average. He sealed the game with two minutes to play when, punting from his own 34-yard line, he sent the ball spinning out of bounds at Notre Dame's 5-yard line.

His teammates carried him from the field.

Iowa and its gritty star were national heroes after the upset, and he clinched the Heisman the following week when he brought the Hawkeyes from a 9–0 fourth-quarter deficit to a 13–9 victory over Minnesota with a pair of touchdown passes. The winning pass was to Green with three minutes to play. "Kinnick 13, Minnesota 9," read the headlines of a Chicago newspaper the next morning.

In addition to winning the Heisman Trophy, Kinnick was picked on every major All-America team; he won the Maxwell and Walter Camp Trophies as the best player in the nation; he topped an Associated Press poll as the nation's top male athlete, ahead of Joe DiMaggio, who batted .381 that season, and heavyweight champion Joe Louis, who knocked out each of his four title challengers.

At a dinner in New York City, Kinnick gave what has been described as "one of the great Heisman acceptance speeches," when he said, in part:

"I thank God that I was born to the gridirons of the Midwest and not the battlefields of Europe. I can confidently say that the boys of this country would rather win this trophy than the croix de guerre."

He played his final game the following summer in the College All-Star Game, passing for two touchdowns and adding four extra points as the Stars lost 45–28 to NFL champion Green Bay. He was drafted by the NFL's Brooklyn Dodgers but spurned their $10,000 contract, a princely sum back then, and embarked on his law school education.

Kinnick finished first in his law school class and then enlisted in the Naval Air Reserve. Nearly four months later—three days before the Japanese attacked Pearl Harbor—he was called to active duty. "May God give me the courage and ability to conduct myself in every situation that my country, my family and my friends will be proud of me," he wrote in a black notebook in which he kept a record of his life.

On June 2, 1943, Kinnick took off in his Grumman F4F Wildcat fighter plane from the recently christened USS *Lexington*, named for the aircraft carrier that had been sunk in the battle of the Coral Sea 13 months earlier. It was a routine training flight in the Gulf of Parla in the Caribbean Sea off the coast of Venezuela.

About 90 minutes into the flight, one of the pilots in his formation noticed oil leaking from Kinnick's engine and led him back to the *Lexington*. The leak had become so serious when he was just four miles from the ship that he had to land in the ocean, a maneuver he executed perfectly. Bill Reiter, the pilot who had escorted him to the ship, later wrote to Kinnick's family that he saw him in the water, free of the airplane, so he then flew back to the carrier to help organize the rescue mission. When the ship reached the site, there was no trace of either Kinnick or the plane, and his body never was found.

Harmon almost met the same fate. He twice was forced out of air corps planes he was flying. Both times he was given up for lost, and both times he eventually walked into the hands of his compatriots with miracle stories of survival.

Of course, they also may be the only time he ever "walked" into success because he forged a great football career at Michigan as one of college football's greatest running backs—a true triple threat when great backs were measured by how much they could do.

Harmon did it all as college football's most feared runner in the late thirties, the only one, to that time, ever favorably compared to the "Galloping Ghost," Harold "Red" Grange of Illinois. "He was superior to Grange in everything but running," said Amos Alonzo Stagg when asked to compare the two. "I'll take Harmon on my team and you can have all the rest."

193

The numbers tell part of the story: for his career, he had 2,338 rushing yards, nearly 6 yards per carry; 33 touchdowns and a like number of extra-point kicks; and 16 touchdown passes. He was the leading scorer in college football in 1939 and 1940. When he won the Heisman Trophy in 1940, he averaged 4.5 yards per carry, his punts averaged 38 yards, his punt and kickoff returns gained a net 17.5 yards each, and he scored 16 touchdowns, 7 on pass receptions.

His 1940 awards tell another part: he won the Heisman Trophy; a second unanimous All-America selection; the Maxwell, Walter Camp, and Knute Rockne Trophies; and his second Big Ten's Most Valuable Player award.

Then there was the running style that made him so deadly on the playing field.

At six feet and 200 pounds, he was a "big back" for his time, but he ran with the grace and ease of someone much smaller. His broken field running was marvelous to watch unless you were a defensive back trying to stop it. He had a wonderful change-of-pace style that simply lost potential tacklers.

He was so good that Forrest Evashevski, the blocking back in Michigan's famed single-wing offense who was his lead blocker for most of his runs, soon gained his own measure of fame. They later starred in the movie *Harmon of Michigan*, one of a genre of films during the forties through which Hollywood glorified the careers of Bruce Smith (*Smith of Minnesota*) and Blanchard and Davis (*The Spirit of West Point*).

Harmon probably won his Heisman Trophy in the 1940 season's first game against the University of California on his 21st birthday. During a 41–0 victory, he scored four touchdowns, including a run of 94 yards with the opening kickoff; a

Tom Harmon.

twisting, 70-yard punt return after muffing the catch and being forced to run back 10 yards to retrieve it; and a reverse run of 86 yards for a third touchdown, stomping over a hapless tackler at the line of scrimmage and then brushing off a last would-be tackler—a California fan who came out of the stands harboring a very bad idea.

Coach Fritz Crisler took him out of the game in the second quarter following his third touchdown. He came back in the fourth quarter to get his fourth score on a basic off-tackle run that he turned into a 65-yard touchdown. He later contributed to Michigan's other touchdown that day with a five-yard scoring pass.

He finished that season against Ohio State almost as he started it, running 25 times for 139 yards and three touchdowns; completing 11 of 12 passes for 181 yards and two TDs; kicking four extra points; returning three kickoffs for 81 yards; intercepting three passes; and averaging 50 yards on each of his three punts.

When he left the game, the 72,000 fans who had jammed Ohio Stadium, nearly all of them rooting for the battered Buckeyes, stood and gave him a huge ovation—a mighty tribute in this rabid rivalry.

Harmon joined the army air forces a month before Pearl Harbor while playing for the Los Angeles team of a short-lived American Football League, after disdaining his selection as the number one choice of the NFL's Chicago Bears. He rose to the rank of captain and was awarded the Silver Star and Purple Heart for valor and heroism.

195

His valor and resourcefulness as an aviator underscored a toughness that was never apparent to those who watched him play football—but it was there nonetheless —because all of his gridiron feats seemed so easy. In one case, a bomber he was flying lost power over French Guiana. He bailed out and into one of the harshest jungle environments in the world. Few thought he would survive, but seven days later, he walked out of the jungle and into a friendly camp.

He flew fighter planes against the Japanese in China and was shot down. He was missing for a month and then presumed dead. But the efforts of friendly Chinese who had formed a survival pipeline to help downed American fliers had saved his life.

But he also paid a horrific price that would cost him his last bit of football fame in the postwar years. The fire aboard his downed fighter plane had badly scorched his legs while he was escaping from the cockpit; the battering he took from his parachute landings had broken his body; and the grueling treks through jungles and rice paddies and up and down mountains took such a toll on him, particularly his famous legs, that his postwar football career with the Los Angeles Rams lasted just two years. He had given everything of his considerable talent to his country.

Harmon later became a renowned sports broadcaster on the West Coast and was one of the first broadcasters to handle national telecasts of college football games. He and his wife, former actress Elyse Knox, were the parents of Mark Harmon, who was a very good quarterback at UCLA in the seventies and later had his own fine career as an actor.

At Notre Dame, Angelo Bertelli and Johnny Lujack were linked almost inexorably in their Heisman Trophy destinies. Both were quarterbacks on Notre Dame's 1943 national champion team. Bertelli started the first six games, and the Irish were 6–0 when his V-12 marine officer training unit was called to active duty. Lujack took over and finished the season, and though the Irish lost their final game in the last 30 seconds to spoil a perfect season, they still were crowned national champions.

Bertelli, even with an abbreviated season, was named the 1943 Heisman Trophy winner after finishing second in 1941 and sixth in 1942. Lujack, who finished third in the 1946 voting, had to wait four years, until 1947, for his honor after he completed the last two seasons of eligibility following duty as a naval officer.

Bertelli, from Springfield, Massachusetts, had resisted the persuasions of Boston College head coach Frank Leahy and enrolled at Notre Dame in 1940. The following season, Leahy came to South Bend as head coach. "He said to me, 'I got you after all,'" Bertelli said years later.

It was a grand alliance. He became Leahy's star tailback in 1941 and helped the Irish to an unbeaten (one tie) season and a third-place finish in the polls. He finished second to Bruce Smith of national champion Minnesota in the Heisman voting.

In 1942, Leahy committed what was thought to be an act of grand treason at Notre Dame—he junked the revered Notre Dame box formation, designed by Knute Rockne and used by every Irish coach who had succeeded him, and switched to the T formation.

"I wouldn't have done it had not Angelo convinced me that he could be an effective T-formation quarterback," Leahy said.

The six-foot, one-inch, 173-pound quarterback didn't do a bad job, winning five games, tying two others, and losing two. Bertelli proved he had the two great skills needed to be a T-formation quarterback: he was very adept at faking the handoffs before delivering the ball to a running back, and his passing skills were just as effective as they had been when he was a tailback. He threw 10 touchdown passes, 4 of them coming against Stanford when he also ran off 10 straight completions.

World War II was at its apex at that time, and every able-bodied young man was subject to military service. The navy had one of its largest V-12 programs at Notre Dame, also offering a Marine Corps option. Bertelli chose the Marine Corps, and he stayed in the program until November 1, 1943, when he was ordered to marine boot camp at Parris Island, South Carolina.

"I was disappointed, but we were at war and we had a lot of patriotic spirit. I didn't even think I'd get to play a down as a senior," he said later. "It happened because a group of us were able to incorporate our marine training as part of the regular curriculum, almost like an ROTC program."

During that shortened 1943 season, he started and won six games, and the team averaged more than 43 points a game. He threw just 36 passes—and completed 25—and 10 of them were touchdowns. In his final game, he led Notre Dame to a

Angelo Bertelli.

crushing 33–6 victory over third-ranked Navy. For the record, the Irish outscored opponents 261–31 with Bertelli at quarterback.

Bertelli didn't know it at the time, but that game nailed down his Heisman, and he was an easy winner over Penn running back Bob O'Dell. He is the only player ever to win the award on the strength of playing just six games. When he sought permission to travel to New York City for the December awards ceremony, it was denied. So the ceremony was postponed until January, when he was granted leave following graduation from Marine Officers School at Quantico, Virginia.

His combat experiences were in two of the bloodiest campaigns of World War II, the invasions of the Pacific islands of Guam and Iwo Jima. They were exclusively marine operations, and, in typical marine fashion, they were won a foot at a time. The invasion of Guam, in June 1944, was part of Operation Forager, which also included invasions of two other islands in the Marianas Group—Saipan and Tinian—all with the objective of establishing long-range bases for air corps B-29s to begin daily bombing of the Japanese home islands.

Bertelli went ashore as part of the III Amphibious Corps, and it took nearly two weeks of combat before the island was secured.

Eight months later, on February 19, 1945, the marines invaded Iwo Jima, the bloodiest island campaign of the war. Bertelli was a replacement platoon leader whose outfit went ashore on the second day of the invasion. Call it the "Luck of the Irish," if you will, but Bertelli missed death or serious injury by 15 feet after a mortar shell exploded in his area. The impact sprayed jagged shrapnel throughout the area, and four marines standing near him were wounded, one seriously. But he didn't suffer a scratch.

Later in the campaign, he wasn't so lucky because a piece of shrapnel tore into part of his shoulder. He was awarded the Purple Heart and a Bronze Star for valor. But what he often remembered most was learning that one of Notre Dame's most fabled players, running back Jack Chevigny, had died in the invasion. According to Notre Dame legend, Chevigny was so affected by coach Knute Rockne's famous "win one for the Gipper" talk at halftime of the 1928 Notre Dame–Army game, that after scoring the lone touchdown to beat Army, he is said to have stood in the end zone and shouted, "That one's for the Gipper."

When Bertelli left Notre Dame for the Marine Corps during the 1943 season, the starting quarterback's job went to Lujack, a young sophomore from Connellsville, Pennsylvania. He had been offered a congressional appointment to attend West Point and play football before Notre Dame coaches even talked to him. But he always maintained that attending Notre Dame had been a boyhood dream, and he secured a scholarship after being invited to the school for a tryout before his high school graduation.

Lujack was a great all-around athlete—a four-letterman in his sophomore year—and coaches said later that he would have been better than Bertelli as a tailback if Leahy had kept the Notre Dame box formation. But when Leahy scrapped that offense for the T formation in Lujack's freshman season, he, like Bertelli, had to learn the new position. He did it so well that at the beginning of 1943, he was Bertelli's backup—but not by much—and played mostly as a backup running back and defensive back until Bertelli left. Later, he also punted and became one of the finest all-around players in the school's history.

"I loved playing both ways, and I hated being taken out of a ballgame," he said. Because his teams were so great, that happened in nearly every game during his varsity career. "You only scrimmaged once a week and you only played nine or ten games. The fun of the game was the competition."

In finishing up the 1943 season for Bertelli, Lujack guided the team to victories in three of its last four games. In his first game as a starter against unbeaten (and pre–Blanchard and Davis) Army, he threw a pair of touchdown passes, ran for another, and set up a fourth with an interception. The Irish won 26–0. In the season's final game, Notre Dame surrendered the winning touchdown in the final 30 seconds against Great Lakes and lost 21–12. Not only did the loss not prevent the Irish from winning the national championship, but the Legend of Lujack had begun.

He was a member of Navy's V-12 program at Notre Dame, and just after his sophomore year ended, in June 1944, he was called to active duty. He was commissioned as an ensign at the navy's midshipman's school at Columbia University, and then he spent the rest of the war serving as executive officer aboard a submarine chaser in the submarine-infested waters of the North Atlantic. It was dangerous duty in perhaps the most turbulent waterway in the world, with constant winter storms roiling the seas and sometimes limiting visibility to a few feet. That made it all but impossible to spot the ever-present Nazi submarine wolf packs that still presented a grave danger to the convoy lanes bringing tens of thousands of American troops and massive amounts of supplies to Europe's battlefields. Later, his ship patrolled the English Channel, helping to keep the supply links open between Great Britain's ports and U.S. forces in Europe.

Lujack returned to Notre Dame before the 1946 season and led what many called the greatest team in the school's history, to that point, to a piece of the national championship with an 8–0–1 record. The only blemish was a scoreless tie against Army's Blanchard and Davis team, in which his tackle of Blanchard saved a touchdown that would have spelled defeat for the Irish. He finished third in the Heisman voting that season.

Incredibly, while planning for the 1946 season, Leahy wanted to put George Ratterman at quarterback and use Lujack as the left halfback. Ratterman was a better ball handler, he had a stronger arm, and he was a wizard at reading defenses. Lujack, Leahy believed, would be more valuable playing as a running back so he could use his great running, passing, and receiving abilities, much as Glenn Davis had done at West Point when he won the Heisman Trophy in 1946.

Those plans fell apart when classroom problems forced Ratterman to leave school and he joined the Buffalo Bills of the newly formed All-America Football Conference.

That didn't deter the Irish from winning a second straight national championship—this one was unanimous—but Lujack established himself for all time as the darling of the Leahy Lads, those dedicated Notre Dame fans who still revere the traditions begun by Rockne and kept alive by most of his successors.

You cannot measure Lujack's success compared to the numbers that today's quarterbacks accrue during a season. In 1947, he completed 61 of 109 passes for 777 yards and nine touchdowns, a three- or four-game total for a Heisman Trophy QB a half century later.

But his passing numbers are not the whole story. He also was one of the nation's best defensive backs that season, and most still believe that the 1947 team was the greatest in the school's history. Forty-two of its members went on to play professional football, and six of them are in the College Football Hall of Fame. The team outscored nine opponents by an average of 32–6 per game. Lujack won the Heisman and every other major award given to running backs and quarterbacks.

A telephone call to the locker room after the Irish had beaten third-ranked Southern California, 38–7, in the season's final game informed him of his winning the Heisman Trophy.

"They said, 'You have to go to New York,' and I said, 'How do I get to New York?' They said, 'Well, you fly.'

"I said, 'I don't have any money for a ticket. How do you get a ticket?' They said they would take care of all that. I had to go across the country, and it scared the life out of me."

Lujack insists that he never gave a thought to winning the Heisman that season.

"No one on our team was into winning awards," he said. "We didn't have the media coverage of now where you could turn on the TV and hear that Johnny Lujack had a good game and was getting closer to winning the Heisman. None of that occurred, and as a result, while it wasn't a total surprise that I won, I didn't know how to explain it.

"That's why I've always considered it as a team award. It would have been ridiculous to think of it any other way."

But for all of the valor and heroism displayed by all of those men, there is something very special and different about 1941 Heisman winner Bruce Smith from the University of Minnesota. He was the star running back of a team that won back-to-back national championships in 1940 and 1941, each with undefeated seasons. Those Golden Gopher teams were the last great college football dynasty before World War II.

Smith was the college football hero whom every fiction writer had concocted long before, and after, he ever played for Minnesota. Some have referred to him as being in the mold of a "classical old-fashioned romantic idol: the team captain, blond, wavy-haired, blue-eyed, with chiseled features and a boyish dimpled smile." As if those drop-dead looks weren't enough, he was a great football player—big and fast, like the other great triple-threat runners of those years, Harmon, Kinnick, and

University of Minnesota running back Bruce Smith.

Sinkwich. All of them were amazing and graceful open field runners or powerful backs who punished defenders between the tackles. They also could pass, kick, catch, and play defense better than any of their contemporaries.

A Chicago sportswriter once wrote: "Bruce Smith even looks like an All-American when he is sitting on the bench."

In 1940, when Michigan and Minnesota met in their famous Little Brown Jug rivalry game, a national championship was at stake between the two undefeated teams. Many saw it as Smith vs. Harmon, not Minnesota vs. Michigan. Late in the first half, Michigan was ahead 6–0 and was about to score again until an interception killed the drive.

On Minnesota's first play, Smith started on a weak-side reverse; before the play was finished, he had run into, around, and through seven Michigan defenders before finishing off an 80-yard touchdown run. The ensuing extra point gave the Gophers a 7–6 lead, and that's how the game ended. It was the third time that season that he had brought his team from behind to a victory by scoring the winning points.

On a personal level, Smith had bested the nation's top player and helped his team to clinch a national championship. But after the game, Smith said, "I feel sorry for Tommy Harmon," alluding to the fact that he feared the loss may have damaged Harmon's chances to win the Heisman Trophy. Of course, it didn't, but Smith's concern was a mirror of his character.

Smith ardently believed that as captain of Minnesota's 1941 team, he had to set the example with how he played and how he comported himself off the field. Though plagued by leg injuries, he insisted on playing, and it often was hard to tell just how badly he was hurt because his efforts never slackened. Against Iowa, Smith did not start the game because of a knee injury. The Gophers didn't gain a yard in his absence. Smith began working on his coach, Bernie Bierman, to allow him to play. Finally, the coach relented, and though Smith carried just nine times that afternoon, it was enough to set up Minnesota's first three touchdowns and lead the team to a 34–13 victory.

Four days before the season's final game against Wisconsin, his chronically injured knees were so bad that he was on crutches and given little chance to play. Four days later, he walked off the playing field with his teammates, 41–6 winners over the Badgers, climaxing the Gophers' second straight unbeaten season and national title.

With World War II underway, Smith enlisted in the navy and spent 1942 at Great Lakes Naval Training Center outside Chicago, where he flashed his Heisman Trophy form as the star of that base's football team. After a rocky start, it became a team so great that it didn't allow a point in six and a half games against such top-level college competition as Missouri, Purdue, Marquette, Illinois, Northwestern, and the first half of a season-ending 13–13 tie against favored Notre Dame. Smith was named Armed Forces Player of the Year in 1942.

Smith entered the navy's aviation program and got his wings, but he did not fly in any combat situations. After the war, he played for the Green Bay Packers and

Los Angeles Rams for a few seasons. He nearly died in a Packers game against the Chicago Bears after a vicious kick in the back ruptured a kidney. He was rushed to the hospital, and his condition was so critical that a Catholic priest administered last rites. He survived, but the chronic injuries that had marred his college playing again caught up to him, and he played only two and a half years in the NFL.

For most of the next 20 years he was a salesman, representing a variety of companies in the Midwest until he was given his own beer distributorship. That enabled him to do what he loved most—stay at home and spend time with his family.

In the spring of 1967, he was diagnosed with terminal cancer. For the next several months, he suffered without complaining as the disease slowly consumed him. Rather than allow himself to wither away, he made a vow to resist the disease so that he could spend one last summer with his family. He died in August.

He also began accompanying a Catholic priest, Reverend William Cantwell, on visits to other cancer patients. Father Cantwell said later that he was unaware of Smith's football achievements but that his courageous suffering and the positive effects he had on the terminally ill children whom he visited were remarkable.

"Everything he did, he did well, including dying," Father Cantwell said. "He had a grace about him. He was gifted. He seldom spoke of his own suffering despite experiencing great pain. He was a great inspiration to the staff and patients of St. Barnabas Hospital in Minneapolis where he received his treatments."

Though he himself was barely 100 pounds—down from 200 when the disease was discovered—the last weeks of his life were so exemplary that there are several in his home state of Minnesota, and in his hometown of Faribault, who have, since his death, believed he should be considered for canonization to sainthood by the Roman Catholic Church. Father Cantwell has always supported their efforts—and for the most basic of reasons: he was unstinting in helping people in their last, desperate hours of need as they battled against the insidious cancers that were wasting their bodies just as he too was fighting his own battle for survival against that terrible disease.

Those who knew him do not find that out of character. For all of his life, but especially during the years when he had national fame as one of college football's great players, he was celebrated as much for his low-key modesty as for his ability to excel on the football field. He was unselfish to those who needed him, be they his teammates at Minnesota or the cancer patients he visited regularly in the final days of his life.

He, like all of the men described in this book, gave the world a supreme act of valor.

Afterword

The message of this provocative book is that valor is a very special trait. It embraces three powerful principles:

Courage: to attempt what you're not at all certain you can achieve.

Selflessness: to risk, personally, so that others may benefit.

And *determination:* to tap deep, uncertain resources to do the seemingly impossible.

As Jack Clary's sagas also illustrate, valor is special, but not rare. I honestly believe it is life's most admirable ideal.

I must confess that I'm not certain the majesty that periodically takes place on Saturday afternoons on those hallowed 100 yards of turf truly constitutes valor. But I *do* believe what takes place there can be an inspiration, and can serve as a revealing guidepost to what true valor is all about. Football—the sport that played such a central role in the lives of the five of us chronicled in this book— is a bright and prominent feature on the landscape of American life. We feel privileged to have been a part of this marvelous sport, as do our teammates and so many others. And we feel doubly blessed to have been chosen for the singular distinction of winning the Heisman Trophy.

Jack Clary's recounting of the highlights of the Academy teams that earned these five Heisman selections, and Joe Bellino's and Roger Staubach's Foreword and Introduction, all reveal the same three themes.

The first of these themes is *team*. It has always struck me as a paradox that the pinnacle award in what is the quintessential *team* sport is one that recognizes *individual* excellence. I suppose that came about because people generally find it easier to identify with the notion of excellence when it is embodied in a specific person. Whatever the reason may be, all five of us recognize the irony of the Heisman. As flattered as we are by the lifelong distinction, we understand even more than most that we are, in fact, simply the standard bearers for a remarkable season and the achievements of all of our teammates.

The second of these common themes is *tradition*. Playing football for Army or Navy ties you into the power of one of the great traditions of the world—the tradition of men-at-arms. (Now, in fact, men *and women* at-arms.) It isn't just the team you're committed to, but to the Academies, as well, and through the Academies to the entire heritage of the military.

I vividly recall an occasion when General Douglas MacArthur spoke to the Army team. In the course of his electrifying pep talk (the most inspirational I've ever witnessed!) he reminded us all of an ennobling truth: That when you step onto the "fields of friendly strife" as a member of the Army team, you play not just for yourself. Not just for the team or the Academy. You play for the honor of the ghosts of a million American soldiers looking down on you who gave their lives for their country!

Call it "the tradition of men-at-arms." Call it "the 12th man." Call it "the long gray line." Whatever you call it, it is a force of incalculable power and strength. And playing for the Army or the Navy, it fuels your every move.

The third theme is *will*. A fundamental truth says, "Nothing worthwhile is easy." That certainly applies to the game of football. The test of rising, week after week, to the emotional level essential to success is daunting. The cumulative effect of an uninterrupted, seasonlong succession of physical drubbings is prodigious. And, to a large extent, only fate determines whether you avoid debilitating injury. Yet the desire for victory somehow overcomes all and, as anyone who has ever played on a championship team knows, it's worth infinitely more than the price of admission.

Is this valor? Perhaps. It certainly qualifies by any work-a-day comparison. It demands courage, selflessness, and determination, to be sure. I would even argue that life lessons of these admirable traits become deeply ingrained through the annealing process of the tough and challenging game of football.

But the stark reality of September 11 reminded us of *another* standard of valor—a standard displayed with stunning clarity on that fateful day and, indeed, one that has been learned and relearned through the years on the battlefields of our nation's wars. As recounted in this book, the standard was exhibited most poignantly by my West Point classmate, Rocky Versace. Held prisoner by his Vietcong captors for almost two years, tortured and sick, confined in a bamboo cage barely as big as he was, he refused to compromise his beliefs or repudiate his country. And on the night before he was executed, alone and in the dark, his fellow prisoners heard his final words as he sang "God Bless America."

Fields of valor appear in many forms. The stakes vary widely, yet the spirit is very much the same. If the Heisman is a metaphor for excellence—which I believe it is—and if the game of football is a crucible of achievement—which it most certainly has become—then that which prompts uncommon commitment and effort, which stimulates drive, determination, and will, and which motivates acts of superhuman effort will in the end produce victory on what can fairly be called a "field of valor."

— Pete Dawkins
New York, New York

Index

208

209

210

211